FLIGHT TO SUCCESS

BE THE CAPTAIN OF YOUR LIFE

AVIATION. INSPIRATION. MOTIVATION.

AT

WWW.KARLENEPETITT.COM

FLIGHT TO SUCCESS

KARLENE K. PETITT

Courtney !
May all you dreams
come true
Karlene Petitt
XO   4/27/2019

JET STAR PUBLISHING INC.
SEATAC WA

ISBN 978-0-9849259-6-4

www.JetStarPublshing.com

Cover Design By Kayla Wopschall

DEDICATION

FLIGHT TO SUCCESS is dedicated to my husband who has shared this journey we call life through turbulence, a few lightning storms, and many sunny days—life has been great, and we are both looking forward to the future. He is literally the wind beneath my wings. Dick, Thank you for being onboard our *Flight to Success*. I love you, for forever and four days.

To my daughters, Kalimar, Kayla and Krysta—there are times I wonder who the teacher is. Thank you all for coming into my life and teaching me how to be a mom. I am so proud of each one of you, and love you very much. Kayla, thank you for another beautiful cover.

To my grandchildren, Kadence, Miles, Kohyn, Carter, Ellis, Anthony and Hayden—you are the joy of any grandmother, and your parents' greatest gift to me. I love you all and will always be there to support your dreams, and encourage you to follow your hearts and many passions in life. The world is yours for the making, enjoy it and be happy. I love you.

To my Mom and Dad, sisters, nieces and nephew—we were all brought together for a reason. It is time to learn to love, forgive, leave the past behind and fly forward to a life we all deserve. Together we are a family and I love you all. Happiness is about choice.

To the inspiration and future of our world, Sydney, Jun, Jeremy, Cecilie, Ryan, Alex, Jeff, Tom, Christine, Dan, Jennifer, Natan, Melissa, John, Adam, Noah, Rachel, Daniel, Holly, Jeff, Joel, Sidd, Katja, Mark, Aisling, Amanda, Anthony, Andrew, Darrin, Dipeet, Emily, Hannah, Jenny, Julia, Lydia, Patricia, Nicole, Ona, Chet, Swayne, Zyola, Tamer, Matt, Sandra, Puja, Karly, Mona, Katie, Alwyn, Parker, Olivia, Balana, and everyone following their dreams—you can achieve anything if you do not quit.

BE THE CAPTAIN OF YOUR LIFE

FLIGHT TO SUCCESS

INSPIRATION, MOTIVATION, AND LESSONS LEARNED.

FLIGHT TO SUCCESS is my journey through eight airlines, seven type ratings, two master's degrees, and motherhood. Intertwined with my stories are those of others who share their successes, failures, losses, fears, hopes and dreams. We have all learned from our experiences. My gift is to share them with you. A key aspect of being a good pilot is compounding experience by learning from others. The best flight tips I've received have come from hangar talk, and from people I've met along the way.

This inspirational, motivational book will take you on the journey of my life to assist you with yours. How did I do it? Why didn't I quit? Where did I find the time, courage, stamina, and strength to persevere during the most challenging times? The answers to these questions and many more will be answered. Each letter in *Flight to Success* represents a motivational chapter that will guide you on your journey.

What drives people to phenomenal success? The secret correlates with many aspects of flight. If you apply these principles to your everyday life there will be nothing you cannot accomplish. Life is about choice. The choice now is to open your mind and heart and begin to dream.

Be prepared to takeoff for the flight of your life, and enjoy the journey.

TABLE OF CONTENTS

FLIGHT TO SUCCESS

WELCOME ABOARD YOUR *Flight to Success*. This book is your ticket to a journey of a lifetime; a journey that will take you to flight levels higher than you have ever experienced, at speeds sometimes beyond your comfort zone, and with visions that can and will become a reality. You no longer have to sit on the sidelines watching others fulfill dreams you wish for yourself. Those successes can be yours if you follow a few life principles. It's time now to preflight your life and get ready to fly.

REDESIGN YOUR METHODOLOGY

I GET HUNDREDS of emails daily asking me how to become a pilot, a flight attendant, or an aeronautical engineer. People tell me they want to write a book, but don't know how to get started and are afraid they'll spend (waste) years writing and not get published. I'm asked what school they should attend, or if they should attend college at all; whether they are too old to start a flying career, how to build flight hours, or if they should change careers. People tell me about their failures, their challenges, their fears, and lack of financial resources. Some ask for advice. Others ask for money. All ask for help. While I do my best to answer everyone's questions, I feel like I'm at an airport trying to get on a flight that keeps changing gates. I'm running from gate to gate, repeating my steps, and climbing on and off the same plane.

Although the emails vary, the underlying questions are the same—how can I achieve success despite the obstacles in my life? What are the best steps to take to achieve my dreams? *I'm afraid*—how do I move forward despite that fear? I'm not sure what I want to do.

Writing individual emails was effective for those who received them, and I was happy to do it. But the reality is that this process was not efficient because the number of incoming email messages continued to increase. Efficiency is essential when you are living a jam-packed life. The best way for me to help everyone was to write a book and answer everyone's questions in one place. Not the end-all, but these are the lessons I've learned on my journey. Now when anyone wants to know how to make their dreams come true, I can tell them, "Read *Flight to Success.*"

Mine and other's stories are included with lessons learned. Our experiences, while some unique, are not uncommon—we have all faced challenges prior to reaching the summit. As you will learn, challenges will be a good thing in many ways. On this journey you will also learn assistance is everywhere once you become committed to your flight.

This book is to help you navigate your personal journey to success as the captain of your life. The skies will not always be calm. In fact, more than often than not, they will be turbulent with strong headwinds holding you back. Rain, sleet, and hail will block your path and sometimes you will have to change course. Fingers of lightning will throw daggers your way and you may find yourself landing at an alternate destination. There will be times your flight may become one of faith. During the darkest days and stormiest nights, you will have to remember the sun is always shining on the other side of the storm.

Whether you are at the beginning of your flight or halfway through your journey, *Flight to Success* will help you achieve your dreams. You don't need to be a pilot to get something out of this book. The secrets I've learned along the way can be applied to achieving anything your heart desires.

Why am I the expert to write this book? I'm not. I am just a normal person who grew up with challenges exactly like yours, desired to move beyond my circumstances to find my place in the world, and wondered at the possibilities of life. My journey was not easy street, but a matrix of routes including multiple flight plans, to get me to where I am today. Was it easy? You tell me. Eight airlines, furloughs, airline bankruptcies, layoffs and mergers were part of my experience. Seven type-ratings, 34 years flying to include 21-years pilot instructing, raising three daughters, being a grandma to seven, married for 34 years, authoring bestselling books, two master's degrees, and pursuit of a PhD in Aviation while editing this book, has not been easy. But it has been fun, and doable. If I can achieve these goals, there is nothing you can't do.

Heading into the second half of my life, having flown airplanes for more than half of the first, I've come to notice a great number of correlations between piloting and success. Perhaps it's nothing more than the necessity of completing the mission. When you're responsible for 300 lives, failure or giving up is not an option. But it's more than that. Being an airline pilot takes training, and so does reaching success. To some, skills come naturally. But to most, we have to work at the process in order to achieve the success we desire.

BE WILLING TO WORK FOR WHAT YOU WANT IN LIFE.

While many people might believe that starting over eight times is a series of unfortunate circumstances, I believe those opportunities were my greatest gifts. Having a career and family was a challenge, but life experiences have been my personal trainer. I have used each lesson for the next challenge. The stories in this book will demonstrate how what might appear to be a failure or setback, is actually the support you need.

THE GREATER THE CHALLENGE, THE BETTER THE LIFE CONDITIONING

As I CONTINUE on my personal journey, with 52 years of con-trails behind me, I'm looking toward the future—a future with abundant success, opportunities, and dreams fulfilled for you, and generations to follow. My goal is to assist you in creating a life of success, fulfilling your wildest dreams, and lifting you to heights that you only thought others could attain. I will share the lessons and observations I learned along the way, but it's up to you what you do with them. If you capture one thing that works for you, then the time spent reading this book was worth it.

LIFE IS ABOUT CHOICE. AND YOU HAVE COMPLETE CONTROL

THIS IS YOUR journey to success and taking notes is encouraged. Stephen King has said, "If you think it, ink it." Create a *Flight to Success* journal—any old notebook will do. Take notes and keep track of your progress. At the end of each chapter of *Flight to Success*, there are exercises to accomplish. Do them. It will be nice to have your work in one place to reflect, or to share with your children one day. This is your story. Grab a pen and paper, and get ready for takeoff.

BE THE CAPTAIN OF YOUR LIFE!

COMMUNICATIVE: Captains listen to their fellow crewmembers, enlisting feedback, and hearing what they have to say. Then they communicate their decisions decisively. They speak loud enough for all to hear, with confidence that they have made the right decision. They create a plan with their crew, and then communicate that plan with dispatch, Air Traffic Control (ATC), and their cabin crew. They tell everyone their intentions. They become accountable. Listen, learn, and communicate along your journey.

ASSERTIVE: Captains know that being assertive with ATC is essential. Assertive is not the same as aggressive, it's strength to say what they want and need. They do not allow controllers to lead them down the path of no return. When a captain is not ready for an approach, he or she asks for radar vectors, or a holding pattern, until they are ready. If dispatch tells them to do something that doesn't feel right, they have the strength to override that decision. Know who you are and what you want in life, and chart your path to achieve it. Own your decisions and outcomes in life.

PREPARATION: Captains are perfectionists in their performance, and know all procedures better than the back of their hand. They know standard operating procedures, set-up procedures, emergency procedures, departure and approach procedures, and with practice will perform them with precision. Knowing what you should be doing is essential to good performance. Be prepared for whatever comes your way.

THINK: Captains think ahead of the plane. They plan for all contingencies before they step into the flight deck. When they brief an abort, they have considered the weather, stopping distance, and any contingency that may limit stopping ability, as well as those that might limit flight. They think beyond the plane. Instead of being reactive, they are proactive in their plans and actions. Create goals and strategies. Evaluate performance and persevere when dealing with all challenges that come your way along your journey. Think before you react.

ATTITUDE: Captains have an attitude of leadership. They are confident, communicative, willing to listen, and support their fellow crewmembers. They are positive, encouraging and appreciate feedback from their team. They know they are not perfect, but always strive to be better than yesterday. Be confident, focused, prepared, and know that life will work out with an attitude of positivity.

INSTILL CONFIDENCE: Captains instill confidence in others by being confident in themselves. They instill confidence by being honest, upfront, and forthright. Trust in yourself and others. Create habits others can count on. Tell the truth to yourself and others.

NOT AFRAID. Captains are not afraid to be human. They know we all make mistakes and they enlist the support of others by making their fellow crewmembers comfortable to speak out if they see something wrong. They are not afraid to say thank you, or to be humble. Be yourself. Know yourself. Never fear stepping into unknown waters, by being prepared.

A man had been visiting a therapist because he feared monsters living under his bed, but the sessions never did any good. Exhausted from being awake each night the man decided to consult another doctor. After one visit he was cured and excitedly returned to his first therapist to tell him the great news. "But we have been working on this for six months," his therapist said. "What did the other doctor tell you?" The man said, "He simply told me to cut the legs off my bed."

CHAPTER 1

FEAR

FRIEND, FOE, AND PERSONAL TRAINER.

"Fear is like fire. It can cook for you. It can heat your house.
Or it can burn you down."
~Cus C'Amato (Mike Tyson's Trainer)

THE MOMENT THE words, "I'm going to be a pilot," tumbled out of my mouth, an overwhelming fear grabbed hold as I gazed into the Boeing 727 cockpit. The number of switches, gauges, and knobs were overwhelming. Three gray-haired men sat at the controls with years of wisdom and experience filling the small space. There was no way I could learn what they knew in order to become a pilot.

Returning to my seat, fear gripped tight as my dream fell to the ground before it had the chance to take off. I had told everyone I was going to become an airline pilot since I was nine-years-old, and those naysayers would say, "I told you so." At thirteen, paralyzed with fear, my world and future were over. I was about to give up my dream, and fall into an abyss of mediocrity with nothing to eat but crow.

YOU CANNOT FAIL IF YOU REFUSE TO QUIT

WHAT MAKES PEOPLE quit before they try? What prevents them from facing life challenges? What gave me the strength to continue my dream despite that overwhelming fear? The same thing that will give you strength to propel you forward—shifting doubt to belief of success!

I had never been on a plane prior to that first viewing of the B727 so of course, the cockpit would be overwhelming. Fortunately my moment of fear occurred on a flight to Disneyland. I spent the next three days submersed in a place where dreams came true. Saturated with possibility, I was brainwashed at a vulnerable time by Walt Disney telling me that I could accomplish anything. I was still afraid, but that fear did not stop me. The power of belief in *myself* pushed me forward. Step one on your *Flight to Success* is to believe in yourself. Make it powerful and strong as if your life depended upon it—because it does.

> *"Believe you can and you're halfway there."*
> ~Theodore Roosevelt

THE DIRECT ROUTE TO SUCCESS

WE HAVE ALL heard, "The road to success is through the door of opportunity." This may be true, but what stops so many people from going through those doors? If it were that easy, why doesn't everyone take opportunities presented? The truth is, it's not that easy because of a secondary barrier, a screen door of fear, blocking the way. The weave on those doors is so fine it's undetectable by the eye, but you feel it. The mesh is tightly woven with feelings, emotions, and excuses. These doors are built with pain, humiliation, and failure you might experience if you were to pass through them. These are the doors of fear blocking opportunity, and we all face them.

To become successful, you must break through this barrier of fear. Unfortunately most people turn and walk away (some run) believing they will find another door at a later date, one that is easier to pass through. But that's not how life works. The screen doors blocking opportunities to success are strong for a reason. They were made by *you* to keep you safe and make you strong. They are made of fear, with fear, and by fear. They were also designed to give you the strength you will need to reach your dreams. You are the architect of these doors, and the greater the opportunity the stronger you will build your barrier.

"Each of us must confront our own fears, must come face to face with them. How we handle our fears will determine where we go with the rest of our lives. To experience adventure or to be limited by the fear of it."
-Judy Blume

The only way you will achieve the level of success you want in life is to learn how to break through your barriers of fear. Great news—the more doors you face and the more often you break through them, the stronger you become. As your strength increases, the power of these doors will weaken and eventually open. It won't be long until all you have to do is give a little push to get through. On the reverse side, if you allow fear to control you, these doors will grow stronger and become more impenetrable as the years pass.

You will always have an opportunity to break through, but the longer you wait, the more difficult facing your fears will become.

Turning away and avoiding challenges will become a lifestyle—a lifestyle built on the habit of allowing fear to control your actions. Besides, more times than not, your fears are nothing more than doubt due to lack of experience. But the only way to gain experience is by living life. Go live it! Each time you break through a door of fear, you will gain experience making the next time easier.

ILLOGICAL LOGIC

WHEN I FACED my first screen door, it slammed closed so hard that it hit me in the face. Fear of not being able to fly because of what I saw in that B727 cockpit was illogical. I did not have to fly the B727 first. Babies learn to walk before they run. Pilots learn how to fly small planes before they fly commercial airliners. Unfortunately when we face fear, illogical logic gets in our way.

Logically I knew that I did not have to jump into a jet and know everything. Logically I knew those pilots started at the beginning. Fear (of the unknown, failure, hard work, logistics, etc.) was the only thing that could derail my career by stopping me from trying. Thankfully my environment at the time saturated me with the belief in myself, and I broke through that first screen door because I pressed on despite the fear.

LIFE'S ANTAGONIST: YOU

ONE OF YOUR greatest antagonists in life will be yourself telling you why you can't do something. Those voices in your head will shout your inadequacies and instill fear. More than that, the world is filled with people that are happy to tell you that you can't do something or you're not good enough—don't be one of them. You are the only person that has control over what you believe. You have the power to tell your inner doubt to shut the f*** up.

For me, timing was perfect and Walt Disney was on my side to squelch my voices of doubt. But you do not need a trip to the happiest place on earth to quiet your voices. You do not need anyone to make you believe how powerful you are—you can do that yourself. Successful people made it because they *believed* they could. They believed in themselves. This belief is something that you have control over. Believe and break through your fear. The more practice you have, the easier it will get.

THE GREATEST FEARS REAP THE GREATEST REWARDS

TWELVE YEARS AFTER that first look into the B727 cockpit, I stood on the ramp staring up at another B727. This time I was scheduled to fly it. *What the hell was I doing?*

As a 24-year-old general aviation pilot with no more than 800 flight hours I had tucked my three babies into bed in Seattle, then flew across the country to Terre Haute, Indiana, chasing the dream of becoming an airline pilot. Navigating training was one thing—you can't die in a simulator. But flying a jet in the current conditions, fatigued, with minimal flight time was another situation all unto itself. Fear stood in my path.

The commute through the night had been long; I was exhausted and afraid. Despite being a mother, I was still just a kid myself with huge responsibilities 2200 miles away. *What if I couldn't handle this life? What if I messed up my kids by being away from home? What if I couldn't fly this plane?* Fear. Fear. And more fear.

My attention shifted to a small plane on final approach. I watched the Cessna bounce like a bronco as if it were trying to throw the pilot. The plane hit the runway sideways on one wheel. It bounced and the engine roared as it crawled back into the sky tossed by Mother Nature. I glanced back at my 170,000-pound jet and then over my shoulder at the operations center. I could turn and walk away—I could run! Was I ready for this? I did not have the experience the other pilots did. I had another life in Seattle that many women would kill for. A voice boomed across the ramp, "Guys, it's time to fly!"

Today is your time to fly

Fly in the face of fear. Successful people are not fearless; they just don't allow their fear to limit what they want and need to do. They are not defined by a lack of fear, but by their relationship *with* fear. Successful people take action *despite* fear. They don't run from their fears, they break through and press forward. When you go through the door of fear, something powerful occurs—you become confident and grow stronger. Inner strength comes from pushing through fear. Courage increases and it's that courage that propels you forward to achieve your dreams. As courage escalates, so does your confidence, and the cycle continues with momentum, enabling you to reach your desired goal. Courage is grown from the seeds of fear and used as a means to success.

> *"You gain strength, courage, and confidence by every experience in which you really stop to look fear in the face. You must do the thing which you think you cannot do."*
> ~Eleanor Roosevelt

Do not confuse courage with being fearless. Courage only grows *from* fear and is earned. There is no room on the flight deck for a fearless crewmember. Fearless people take risks without thinking. This may give them an edge in some circumstances, but fearless people are often irresponsible. They will fly into weather that should be avoided, or jump into a pool not knowing how to swim. The fearless might get away with whatever it is once in a while, but their recklessness will eventually catch up to them. Fearless people make poor decisions, which do not lead to long-term success. Many general aviation accidents have been attributed to reckless behavior.

> *"There are old pilots and bold pilots,*
> *but no old, bold pilots."*
> ~E. Hamilton Lee

SPAR WITH FEAR

FEAR IS A personal trainer on your journey to success. Facing fear and taking action in spite of it, is similar to lifting weights. Each time you lift, you become stronger. As you grow stronger, you will be able to add more weight. Facing fear and vulnerability strengthens your soul, your character, and your potential.

> *Life is a weight-lifting bar—*
> *always add a little more than you are comfortable with.*

PREPARE FOR THE NEXT BIG CHALLENGE

THERE WILL *ALWAYS* be challenges in your life. Sometimes they will be disguised as opportunities and other times they will come across as unfortunate circumstances. But they will show up and you will have to deal with them. The question is—what will you do? Run? Hide? Avoid? Or face them? I am not talking about running unprotected into a fire. The fear I'm talking about are those opportunities that are passed-by because of the *excuses* you make as to why you can't do something.

I stood on the ramp below that B727 because I faced a greater fear months earlier. Evergreen Airlines offered me a job well before I anticipated going to work as a pilot. My daughters were only two, three and four-years old, and I was planning for my career to begin when they were in school. But when Evergreen called and asked if I wanted a job I said, "Yes!" They asked if I minded being based in Terre Haute. I said, "No problem." We said our goodbyes, I hung up the phone, and then reality hit—I couldn't take the job, and where the heck was Terre Haute?

SAY YES TO OPPORTUNITIES

THERE WAS A pattern setting up early in my life—take the challenge, then figure out the rest later. We get one first impression, but we also get one first chance to show how much we want an opportunity. There is always time to contemplate later, but when someone asks if you want a shot at your dream, there is only one answer—when do I start!

So I snagged the career of a lifetime with minimal flight time. Then fear smacked me in the face, as did all the reasons why I should not have accepted this job. My kids were too young. The offer came three years before my plan. *Who would take care of the family while I was gone? Who would take care of the house? The yard? Would everyone eat? How could I leave my family days and weeks at a time?* My excuses were endless. Not only were my excuses endless, I had family and friends *implying* I was not a good mother, questioning how could I leave my kids when *they* would never do such a thing.

When we fear, we make excuses—a validation system to give credence as to why we are willing to bypass an opportunity. We also justify our decision by saying that if this chance came now, it surely will come again. *Will it?* Sometimes there is only one chance. But more than giving up the opportunity itself, when you don't break through that door because of fear-based excuses, you are giving up an opportunity to grow.

Having voiced all my concerns to my husband as to why I could not take this job, he said, "Opportunities like this come along once in a lifetime. If you want to be a pilot, we will make this work." He was right. I had the opportunity and the reality was, there would never be a *good* time. Excuses could flow no matter how old the kids were, and whatever life stage we were in.

ASSESS YOUR EXCUSES

WHEN YOU FIND yourself making excuses as to why you are not willing to take action, take a serious look at what you're saying and ask yourself why you're saying it. Identify the real reason—not the excuse. The underlying reason will undoubtedly be fear based. Valid as your excuses are, could you make it work? More than likely the answer will be yes.

Thus we made a plan and off I went into the first real airline job of my career. My fears did not diminish. I went *despite* those fears. After my initial training, I headed to Terre Haute, Indiana, for the final test. The entire class needed to fly the plane prior to being released for duty. This was a test for me in more ways than one. When I heard, "Guys, it's time to fly!" I sucked down my fear, smiled, and climbed aboard that B727. The biggest plane I had flown prior to this was a Cessna 402. I had 5000 hours less than the next lowest-time pilot in my class. *Could I do it?* Rational logic said—I was trained to fly this plane. I would not have been signed-off and put in the cockpit if I wasn't ready. Was I afraid? *Oh yeah.* I climbed in and buckled up—power set and moments later we were airborne.

I focused *only* on flying the plane—not the kids at home, not my husband, not *what if* I failed. There is a time and a place for every thought. The time now was to focus on flying, not on the fear of what if. Little did I know that this experience would be the first of many opportunities to face fear. Yes—it does get easier.

IF YOU DID IT BEFORE, YOU CAN DO IT AGAIN

THE POWER OF pushing through fear provides the experience to know that you can do the unimaginable. You did it before—you can do it again. There is great power and confidence derived from experience. My first airline job was more than an opportunity to begin a flying career. That first job was a life lesson on the power of facing fear. This relationship with fear is what has enabled me to achieve success in all areas of my life.

> *Build a relationship with fear*
> *to conquer your fears, not run from them.*

As A JUNIOR in high school I ran for vice president because I was afraid of talking in front of people and wanted to push through that feeling. Running for office forced me to give a speech to the entire student body. I took classes that required me to stand in front of the room and talk to my peers.

Thirty-six years after that first speech I sat in the green room, ready to go live on CNN. My heart beat rapidly and I thought— *what in the heck am I doing?* I was scared to death. With a huge grin, I shrugged it off knowing that one of two things would happen—I would look like a fool, or not. It was as simple as that. I'm sure I have looked like a fool before and more than likely, I will again. I can live with looking foolish, but not with giving up opportunities because I was afraid, and later end up wishing I *would have taken the opportunity.* This is a choice you need to make for yourself—choose to face your fears.

POWER OF EXPERIENCE

WHILE THERE HAVE been many fears along the way, the most recent for me was in early 2014 as I was about to embark on my next big challenge—navigating a PhD program at Embry-Riddle Aeronautical University. There were many reasons as to why I should not have undertaken that challenge. *What if I failed because I wasn't good enough? What if I couldn't find the time to do the work? What if I was too old and my brain couldn't absorb new data? It was so expensive. I had to take the GRE (Graduate Record Examination). I'm busy and have books and movies to write!* My response to those excuses—I've faced these fears and others throughout my life and I have always made it work. *Why not now?* I pushed fear aside, and went through the door.

There is rarely a time when I try something new that I don't feel a tickle of fear. But I do not allow those feelings to control me, and each time the challenge gets easier for one reason—my experiences have taught me that everything works out. There have been many dark tear-filled nights along my journey, with pain, sorrow, sickness, and loss—there will be for you as well. But those, too, have a way of working out if you don't fear feeling the pain, crying the tears, and dealing with what might seem like the impossible. You are more capable that you could ever imagine, and your strength will grow through fears of all kinds.

PUSH YOURSELF TO THE EDGE

NOW IS YOUR time to start creating the life you desire. Push yourself to the edge. Fear is nothing more than an emotion stemming from the unknown—an unknown audience, an unknown airplane, unknown questions at an interview, unknown performance, and so on. A secret about the unknown is that these unchartered experiences are the fun part of life. I'm not jumping out of planes or climbing cliffs, because I have no desire to do those things. But I am taking steps into the world of new experiences when challenge calls my name—despite my fear. Along the way I am building confidence for the next adventure. What happens if you take the challenge and fail? Feel proud because you tried, get over it and move on.

LIFE HAS PLANS ALL ITS OWN

LIFE DOES NOT always work out like we think it should. There will be times when the wind blows you off course. Don't fear the wind, use it to your advantage and make appropriate heading changes. Use the wind to provide lift. When life blows open the doors of opportunity, go through them. Take action despite your fears.

If I had not stood in front of the most challenging audience of my life—high school students—would I have been able to say yes to CNN? Speaking of which, the third time was so much easier than the first. You will never get to the third until you live through the first. You have to risk looking foolish and making mistakes along the way.

Be prepared. Be safe. But live your life in the game, not on the sidelines.

RESPECT FEAR

FEBRUARY OF 1996 found me standing in Saudi Arabia with a Tower Air captain in an open-air market called a souk. We walked into a jewelry store and I found myself fascinated by the wealth of jewels glimmering in the cases. A diamond and emerald necklace caught my eye, valued at $250,000. The salesman removed this gem from behind the glass. He held it out and said, "You try. Take outside and see how beautiful." Holding up both hands I said, "No thank you."

"Please," the man said, insistent. "Will be so beautiful. Please take look in sunshine…" he added, shoving the jewels into my hands. Something *felt* wrong. "I looked him in the eye and said, "No. Thank you," shoving them back into his hands. Later I shared that story with our liaison, and how impressed I was that they trusted nobody would steal. His reply, "He did not trust you. He was setting you up. Had you gone outside he would have yelled, "Thief!" and you would have been imprisoned." Not only would I have been imprisoned, had the other pilot not known where I had gone, I would have received no food and water, or been allowed a call.

Fear is your personal trainer in life to make you stronger. But there are times that you must listen, as it could save your life. The confusion arises as how to distinguish between fear that you should avoid to keep you safe, and fear you should press through to achieve success. For me, the answer comes down to feeling or thinking.

If I *feel* something is not right—I feel it in my gut. Hairs stand up on the back of my neck. I hear my inner voice giving me guidance (not excuses). I don't feel right about whatever it is… These are the messages of warning. When I *feel* fear, I honor it. This is different from when my *mind* jumps in and makes excuses based on *what if* I don't succeed. Who would cook and clean were clearly head-based thoughts, and did not come from the gut—maybe somebody's gut, but not mine. If I *think* things such as what if I look foolish, what if I fail and have to eat crow, etc., I know my fear is one to be faced. If it *feels* wrong, it probably is wrong. If I *think* up excuses, this is a fear I need to meet head on.

I also avoid fear-based situations that have a probability of killing me. If you face a situation that could kill you and you feel fear, be cautious of your other excuse system of rational-ization—that time when you make up excuses to devalue your feelings. Many planes have crashed when someone had a feeling that something was wrong and ignored it. Becoming in tune with what your body is telling you grows with awareness, and through that awareness you *will* know right from wrong. How many times have you thought, *maybe I shouldn't do this*, and it came back to bite you because you did it anyway? That is the gift of fear keeping you safe.

LEAVE FEAR BEHIND

AFTER YOU FACE your fear and break through the door, leave your fears behind. If you push through fear but *think* about what you feared while doing what you were afraid to do—you will get what you feared. This is the power of focus and concentration. Many years as a simulator instructor have shown me that those who focused on the fear of failure, and not on what they were doing, reaped the rewards of their thoughts.

When you face your fears, do not look back. Do not think about them. Once you become committed to taking off, make it morally, legally and ethically wrong to carry that fear with you. You found the courage to break through your fear, find the courage to leave the negative thoughts behind you. Do not think *what if* while you are doing. While flying my jet, I focus only on flying the plane—not on my family, not on the passengers, not on the check airman sitting behind me, or what if I do a bad landing.

One of the most powerful tools in your flight bag is your ability to leave fear on the ground and focus on the task at hand. Focus on where you are going, not what can stop you. You are headed toward success. The first step is pushing through your fear, taking flight, and leaving the safety of the runway behind.

"Everything you want is on the other side of fear."
~Jack Canfield

TAKE ACTION NOW

- List one situation (or more) that you fear. Speaking in front of a group? Asking someone on a date? Applying for a job? Flying a plane? Singing Karaoke? Publishing a book?
- Select a fear and face it. Begin to break down those doors so when you are ready for the big time, they will be easier to open.
- Watch the movie *42*—the story of Jackie Robinson. Success comes from facing your greatest fears.
- Read the book *The Gift of Fear* by Gavin De Becker. His lessons could save your life.

Marc was a photographer for *The Seattle Times*, and was scheduled to meet a plane on the tarmac to take him for a photo shoot. He glanced across the ramp and saw a pilot sitting in a plane, and approached. "Ready to fly?" Marc asked. "As ready as I'll ever be," the pilot said.

Marc waited impatiently, and then asked, "Well? Are we going to get going?" "What do you want me to do first?" the pilot asked. "How about we get flying and go from there?"

The pilot sucked deep breath and taxied to the runway, and was soon airborne.

"OK," Marc said, "Fly around the Space Needle and then low over Puget Sound I want to take a few pictures."

"What do you mean?" the pilot asked.

Annoyed, Marc looked at the pilot and said, "I need to take some pictures for the *Times*, so please..."

There was a long pause, and the pilot said in a shaky voice, "You mean you're not my flight instructor?"

CHAPTER 2

LISTEN AND LEARN

"The most important thing in communication
is hearing what isn't said."
~Peter Drucker

SKIES WERE CLEAR as I sucked the landing gear up and headed toward the Cascades in a Cessna 182RG. It was fall of 1985 and class was done for the day, but life's lessons were about to continue. I was on my daily commute home from Ellensburg, Washington, to Renton airport. This was my final quarter before graduating from Central Washington University.

To accommodate family, time constraints, and building hours, I sometimes flew myself instead of driving. My plane had great performance as she climbed to 8500 feet with ease. Snoqualmie pass slept silently under a cloud layer and I scooted over the top. Off to my left, Mount Rainier stood a little over 14,000 feet as I skated down an airway toward home. "Cessna 4972 Tango descend and maintain 7500 feet," blared over my radio speakers. I replied to the clearance and descended into the clouds. I had an instrument rating and was on an instrument flight plan so this should not have been a problem. But it was.

The freezing level and I were at the same altitude and within seconds ice attacked the windshield and grabbed the control surfaces. It grew rapidly and clung to my plane. The propeller beat off the attack, but was losing the battle. Planes don't fly with ice coating their surfaces and I could no longer climb above the weather. I was stuck as ice accumulated and airspeed dropped. It wasn't long until my plane could no longer sustain lift, and I was losing altitude.

Searching for a solution, my tickle of concern was met with a realization that I was far enough over the pass and descent into warmer temperatures was within reach. I requested a lower altitude. Ice melted. My plane flew. I lived and learned. My flight lesson for the day—don't let air traffic control (ATC) fly your plane. Equally as powerful was life's lesson—the lesson of the experience.

We all make errors in judgment based on the best knowledge we have at the time. These lessons are gifts if we live through them. They are gifts to others if we share them. Sometimes they come with a cost. This is the primary reason pilots need flight hours—to gain experience. But experience that does not make an impact is another lesson waiting to happen. Life success depends upon how well you listen to the messages associated with your experiences. You must learn from them, because you will be tested again.

Ultimate success depends upon your ability to learn

I paid attention to what happened that day early in my flying career. I had allowed someone else to make a command decision of my plane, which may have been my last flight. Granted ATC has the right and responsibility to provide clearances. However, that controller was not in my plane and I should have said,

"Unable due to weather. I would like to remain at altitude for another thirty miles."

I have shared this story with hundreds of students over the years because experience belongs to the world. I have learned a great deal from others along my journey, as I hope you will learn a few lessons in this book. On your journey to success, make a commitment to listen and learn something from everyone you meet.

> *Experience is a gift that you receive*
> *and share with others.*

This was a challenging chapter title, as I contemplated which was more essential to success—listening or learning. Reality is they run parallel on the level of importance. You don't need a head-pounding to learn life's lessons. All you need is to listen to the messages and learn the lessons associated with each one as they occur.

LISTEN ACTIVELY

LISTENING IS MORE than just hearing, it comes down to understanding what is being said—the essence of an education. Unfortunately active listening has become a lost art. People are so busy they half-listen and miss the essence of what is being spoken. Messages and teachers are everywhere, pay attention. During your journey to success, become aware of all lessons presented—written, spoken, experienced, and stories from others.

When I was young, my mother told me to respect my teachers. She also said, "Just because your teachers say something doesn't mean they are always correct. Be respectful, but keep your mind open to other possibilities." My interpretation of her wisdom was to be inquisitive, not doubting, and I have lived my life accordingly. Her advice has worked well for me, and it will for you too.

When something is spoken that doesn't resonate, dig deeper, looking for the truth, and ask questions. Don't *distrust* what people say, listen and validate—trust but verify. Active listening will always lead to learning. Those you listen to might not always be right, but everyone has something to teach you, as does each moment of your life.

We have two ears and one mouth because we were meant to listen twice as much as we talk. Practice paying attention while others are speaking. If you are thinking about a reply while someone is talking, you are not actively listening and a communication breakdown is in the making. Your ability to communicate effectively will lead to success in all areas of your life.

LEAVE YOUR CAPE AT THE GATE

BE OPEN TO what others are saying as they may be sending you information that will be beneficial to your success. On your journey, be absolutely confident that you *do not* know everything. Once you understand that, you will be more willing to listen. The worst students, and pilots alike, are those who think they know everything.

> *"Wisdom is the reward you get for a lifetime of listening when you'd have preferred to talk."*
> ~Doug Larson

The primary reason people don't listen to others is their ego gets in the way. Ego is not a bad thing, and perhaps is one of an airline pilot's most valued strengths. We want those people who hold our lives in their hands to be confident. There is no doubt that successful people have strong egos. A healthy ego combined with a sense of self is essential on your journey to success. But when your ego becomes so big that you think you know everything, you have set your flight on a route to failure. Keep the super-powers during your journey, but leave the cape at the gate.

Do not mistake an overinflated ego with confidence. When your ego convinces you of your greatness, you will stop listening and growing. The "I am wonderful and you can't tell me anything," ego can turn a headwind into a tailwind on departure, in a matter of seconds. Planes takeoff into the wind for a reason—performance. Once en route, a tailwind will push you along faster, but first you must get flying. An untamed ego, like that departure tailwind, exceeds limitations. You won't fly. On this journey to success, tame the beast and use your confidence to listen and learn.

"Courage is what it takes to stand up and speak; Courage is also what it takes to sit down and listen"
~Sir Winston Churchill

OPEN YOUR MIND TO POSSIBILITY

THOSE UNWILLING TO listen to others have closed their minds to the wisdom that could accelerate their journey. Not only does learning halt but closed-minded people also become unapproachable and communication stops. Many airline crashes have been attributed to a captain who created an atmosphere of being inaccessible. The resulting intimidation left crewmembers silent to their deaths. If an airplane can crash because a captain believes he knows everything and nobody is willing to tell him when something is wrong, how do you think that attitude will impact your chance of success?

BE TEACHABLE

SUCCESSFUL PEOPLE ARE open to the education they receive along their journey by listening to others. While we often associate education with formal schooling, education comes in many forms.

The best life lessons come from the classroom of experience while listening to what the world is shouting in your direction.

When I finished my first novel, I asked one of my favorite authors, Robert Dugoni, if he would read it for an endorsement. After reading *Flight For Control* he said, "I loved your book, but I did not like the ending and here is why..." Then he added, "I'm sure this is not what you wanted to hear, but had I not enjoyed the story I would not have made it to the end."

My response was, "It's not what I'd *hoped* to hear, but it's exactly what I *needed* to hear." A fabulous discussion ensued and I rewrote the final chapter. When I thanked him, he said, "It's a pleasure to work with someone who is *teachable*." Because I was able to push my ego aside, I was able to write the ending that my novel deserved. Be teachable.

You are writing your story—it's called your life—your journey to success. There are people everywhere sharing gifts of knowledge that can help you. If you are willing to listen, these morsels will help you achieve your dreams.

Teachers will appear when you need them

I had just checked out on the Airbus A330. During each of the following three months, I flew with a captain who had something to teach me. The level of what they taught me was an upward stair-step based on my ability, each month growing to the next level. The teachers appeared as I needed them. By month three I was feeling good about the plane, and then the next life teacher arrived. He said, "Have you kicked everything off and flown the plane yet?" Then added, "I would recommend you do this sooner than later."

Kick everything off meant flying the plane without automation. Up to this point, I had yet to witness a pilot disengage the autopilot until the last five hundred feet, yet they kept the auto-thrust engaged. Not even during my line training with a check airman did I disconnect the autothrust. How scary is that in an Airbus—the thrust levers don't even move! I'm joking. They may not move by themselves, but we have the power to add and reduce thrust just like any airplane.

During the last leg with this captain, I glanced left—there was no better time than to do this than with the captain encouraging it (my life teacher) sitting beside me. Waiting until 10,000 feet I allowed the airplane to slow, then *kicked everything off.* At that moment, I felt like I was on a checkride. ATC fired command after command.

"Turn left to a heading of 270. Slow to 230. Descend 2000 feet. Slow to 210. Turn farther left to a heading of 265." We were in the clouds and the plane bounced, as did the trend vector on the speed tape; up and down it flew wildly while I attempted to maintain speed. Finally we broke free of the clouds, the bumps smoothed out and the captain said, "I'm surprised you did that." I said, "But you encouraged that type of behavior." He said, "Yes. In visual conditions."

Clearly I missed that part of that communication. But I used the opportunity to do what he said, kick it off, which gave me the confidence and experience to fly my plane without automation. If I could handle the process in the conditions we had been in, visual conditions would be a piece of cake.

There are times when those who teach us are not accurate. But unless we're willing to listen, we'll never know. The month prior a captain shared his knowledge of the plane across the Atlantic—I learned a great deal. Then he asked, "How are your landings?" I said, "Great." (I had not been on the plane long enough to over think it.) He then proceeded to tell me how to make the *perfect* landing.

His technique was to visually 'stay inside' (on the instruments) until 50 feet. Up to this point, at 100 feet I transitioned outside and looked down the runway glancing in and out. At 50 feet I was already thinking about the landing, tickling the stick, and at 30 feet I began feeling for the flare to stop the descent. But I was willing to try anything that could give me the *perfect* landing *every* time.

Unfortunately that 'anything' after being awake for 17 hours, with delayed reaction time due to fatigue, manifested to staying inside until 50 feet and then a second later my saying, "Oh shit!" as I looked outside. With a 700 foot per minute descent and a 50-foot wakeup call, there was not a lot of room to manage that transition to the runway. My eyes flashed outside and down the runway that my plane was about to become friends with very quickly.

After impact the other first officer said, "I thought it was going to be harder." The captain said, "I have seen worse." My thought… *Of course you have, and I'm never doing that again!* Two days later it was my landing again, and he told me to do the same thing—stay inside until 50 feet, and I said, "Okay." I didn't, of course. When the landing was awesome, he said, "See how great that works."

There are times when we listen and learn. There are other times we learn what not to do. We also learn when to keep our mouths shut—I say this smiling because we had hours of dialogue about landing, en route. He was adamant that his way was the only way. Another lesson to success—some things are better left unsaid, especially if there is someone not willing to listen and learn. As my youngest daughter told me years ago—smile and nod. Then do the best you can.

We can learn something in every situation and with every person we meet. But *only* by maintaining an open mind and parking the ego outside will we be able to identify truth from opinion and fact from fiction. A challenge in life will be to have that open mind, grab what works and when something doesn't feel right, or that landing is hard, find your own truth. Find what works best for you. But always listen to the messages around you.

Every person you meet, experience you live through,
and every opportunity that presents itself
is a learning moment waiting for you to embrace it.

One night I was flying an A330 from Tokyo to Seattle. My fellow first officer and I were in the flight deck the last couple hours of our flight, during the captain's break. I learned that he had a passion for teaching and had an aviation safety background. During the ensuing discussion, he told me about three books to add to my must read list. With a dozen unread books on my desk, I certainly did not need one more, let alone three. I could have made all the excuses in the world why *not* to buy them. But the point is, I've become keenly aware that we get what we need in life. This is the gift I'm giving to you—create awareness and listen.

My being called out last minute for this particular flight, and this pilot being rescheduled due to a hydraulic failure on his previous flight, put us in a plane together that was not a scheduled trip. Multiple events occurred to bring us together, and I used the message that there was something to be learned from this person, and perhaps it was in the books he recommended.

These types of events are something that will happen to you as you progress on your journey to success. When you allow life to unfold and become aware of the messages coming your way, you are more apt to listen and pay attention. I'm better at paying attention than I used to be. Perhaps the sore head from that sledgehammer has helped to create awareness. I ordered the books.

After reading the first, *Deep Survival: Who Lives, Who Dies, and Why*, the question as to why we were brought together was answered—I needed that book. This was one of the best books I had read in a long time. The correlation to success and survival cannot be missed. As it turns out, the research that had gone into this book is something I will use as I continue on my journey with education in aviation safety.

You have something to learn

"The teacher is the one who gets the most out of the lessons, and the true teacher is the learner."
~Elbert Hubbard

MANY YEARS AGO America West Airlines hired me as a simulator instructor with a fresh type rating and only 2 hours of actual flight time on the B737. Many of the pilots I was teaching had far more experience than I. How could education occur in this scenario? More accurately, who was the teacher and who was the student?

Having learned procedures and systems from training manuals, and knowing how to operate the simulator was a start. The rest I learned from the experience of my students. I took from the line captains and gave to the new-hire students. If I saw a captain performing a technique, I asked him about it. If there was value, I used his experience and passed that on to my next student. I learned from my students and shared the wealth. Others' knowledge has always been part of my teaching tool kit.

By listening, questioning, and understanding what was happening on the flight line, I was able to accelerate my learning through the experiences of others. This process not only made me a better instructor, but it also showed me the power of compounding an education.

Teaching is sharing knowledge
Learning is gathering knowledge

While flying for an International Airline, I was in the process of earning a master's degree in human services and one of my daughters said, "Why are you going to school, you already have a job?" Great question.

The average person will educate him or herself because they have to, not because of what they can learn. They go to college because a four-year degree is required. They take the weekend instrument course to pass the written test. They take classes because they are required. If you want a life filled with success, push away from the average—become unique. Learn something because of the education you will receive.

We live in a society where we *do* because we *get*. Not to say that behavior is wrong, but the focus lies on the 'get' at the end of the task, not on what we learn along the way. While we might associate achieving a degree as a quotient of success, the education attained is far more important. What you learn will carry you farther than the diploma on your wall. By shifting your thinking to what you might learn versus getting that 'A', the education you receive is what you will use in your flight bag of success.

"Education is what remains after one has forgotten what one has learned in school."

-Albert Einstein

CREATE A LOVE OF LEARNING

A MASTER'S DEGREE in human services was followed by a master's degree in business management. You might think I enjoy attending school, but that was not always the case. I did minimal in high school, took easy courses and wanted to get out and on with my life. My attention was on learning how to fly, not history or math. I had no idea what was available to me back then. I had no idea of the opportunities that I allowed to slip past. Live and learn. Today I wake up and ask, "What can I learn today?"

A love of learning will accelerate your level of success. This has nothing to do with having the most knowledge—there are a lot of educated idiots walking the earth. Wisdom and how you use that knowledge is the key to success. When you focus on learning as the goal, versus the degree you pin to your wall, your mind shifts from the fear of making mistakes, to one of looking forward to them because of what you will learn. Focus on what you can learn, not the degree. Grades are a great benchmark and it's fun to receive that letter A, since you don't live in the 17th century in Boston, but it's the education that's the gift that will be used throughout your life, focus on that!

BE WILLING TO ASK QUESTIONS

PILOTS RECEIVE A briefing from dispatch concerning weather and routing. The captain briefs the flight attendants. Pilots brief each other. We are not just wagging our lips. We are sharing information that is pertinent to our flight, and creating expectations of how we will operate so we are all on the same page. At the end of every brief someone asks, "Does anyone have any questions?" I cannot imagine a flight where we don't listen and learn from each other. I cannot imagine a life without asking questions.

In aviation, questions are rampant. Pilots want clarity. If we don't understand something, we ask. When the instructor wants to assess knowledge, they ask a question. Questioning has always been a huge part of my life as an instructor and when operating aircraft. So you can imagine my surprise when I heard that questions were not allowed.

During my first writers group, we would read, edit, and offer suggestions to each other. One woman commented about something I had written and I wanted to know why she felt the way she did. Instead of answering my question she said, "That's not how this works. You don't get to ask questions. You just take the opinion and either use it or don't!" This is not an attitude that will work well in your life. Vote people off the island with that opinion.

You cannot learn if you don't understand what you don't know. Questions are essential in the process of learning. Listening to what is being asked is equally as important. This writer's group was not my first experience where questions were not allowed. Many years ago I was invited to teach two Chinese pilots on the B737, with the aid of an interpreter—the pilots did not speak English and I did not understand Chinese. I was not exactly sure how the process worked. Did I ask the pilots questions and the interpreter would listen and relay? Or did I speak to the interpreter directly, and then she would communicate what I had asked? When I posed those questions to the training center manager he said, "No! The instructor *never* asks questions. You tell them what they need to know." As it turned out, they did not ask questions either.

How did I know what they knew? I didn't. How did I know if they understood? I didn't. This *no question* process was inefficient and unsafe, and one of the primary culture issues of foreign airline crashes. Thankfully, lacking the power to question is not standard protocol in the US aviation industry.

> *"A wise man's question contains half the answer."*
> ~Solomon Ibn Gabirol

Whether you are a pilot or not, take an aviation gift with you—it's okay to question. And for those of you questioned, do not assume you are being challenged. Respond with the intent that the person wants to learn. A learning moment might occur for everyone. It's okay to say, "Wow, I had not thought of that before." There is a reason pilots share their experience with me. I ask questions and have a love of learning. When meeting pilots who are aligned with this sharing mentality, we have great discussions. I always learn something.

DIALOGUE. LISTEN. BE OPEN TO LEARNING.

LEARN TO LISTEN actively on your journey to success. These skills are as essential as if you were on a plane copying a clearance. The key to learning is your willingness and humility to know that you don't know everything. There is so much we can all learn and the world is our university if we listen to the messages along the way. The most successful people know how to listen and embrace the power of education. This power of listening will enhance the learning process. The rest is up to you.

> *"Live as if you were to die tomorrow.*
> *Learn as if you were to live forever."*
> ~Mahatma Gandhi

TAKE ACTION NOW

- Practice active listening.

- Pay attention to life as it unfolds. What did you learn today? Make a habit of learning something new each day and write the lesson in your notebook.

- Make life a Google search by asking the right questions. Instead of saying, "Why does this always happen to me?" ask, "What do I need to learn from this situation?" The answers arrive when you ask the right questions.

- Watch the movie *Karate Kid*—a story of a young man who finds his way from the life lessons given by his neighbor. Who is your teacher and what can you learn today?

The chief of staff of the US Air Force decided that he needed to intervene in the recruiting crisis affecting all armed services. He directed a nearby Air Force base to be opened for enlistment, and that all eligible young men and women be invited to apply.

As he and his staff stood near a new F-15 Fighter, twin brothers who looked like they had just stepped off a Marine Corps recruiting poster walked up.

The chief of staff stuck out his hand and introduced himself. "Son, what skills can you bring to the Air Force?" The young man looked at him and said, "I pilot!" The general, turned to his aide and said, "Get him in today!" The aide hustled the young man off.

The general looked at the brother and asked, "What skills can you bring to the Air Force?" The young man said, "I chop wood!" "Son," the general replied, "We don't need wood choppers in the Air Force."

"Well," the young man said, "You hired my brother!" "Of course we did," says the general, "He's a pilot!" The young man replied, "But I have to chop it before he can pile it!"

CHAPTER 3

IDENTITY

WHO ARE YOU?

KNOW THYSELF

"We have to really educate ourselves in a way about who we are, what our real identity is."
                                          ~Deepak Chopra

MARC MEDLEY WAS about to enter college and wanted to major in either English or music, but his father was not supportive of either choice due to a lack of financial opportunities after graduation. His father had told him if he wanted to be a successful entertainer, Marc would have to be someone like Michael Jackson. If he majored in English he would have to teach, and teachers did not make very much money. Thus Marc majored in business.

The largest telecommunications company in the world hired him. He worked for that company for fifteen years and moved up the corporate ladder. To others, he had achieved great success. But to Marc, something was missing. He wasn't passionate about going to work—he needed more. In search of the thing that excited him, he began teaching in the evenings at a local college. Marc subsequently found what was missing—the essence of who he was—a passionate educator. He passed the required teaching tests, and shortly thereafter left the corporate world behind to become a fulltime teacher at a fraction of his previous salary.

THIS IS YOUR LIFE—OWN IT

> *"Your time is limited, so don't waste it living someone else's life. Don't be trapped by dogma—which is living with the results of other people's thinking. Don't let the noise of others' opinions drown out your own inner voice. And most important, have the courage to follow your heart and intuition."*
>
> ~Steve Jobs

LIVING SOMEONE ELSE's life is like losing your navigation system and having a passenger tell you where to go. You will end up someplace, but not *your* destiny—definitely not your destination called success. When passengers tell the pilots where to go it's called a hijacking. Do not allow anyone to hijack your life.

Many people like Marc lose their voice because they were encouraged to pursue their parents' choice of a career. I get it—you want them proud of you and they might be paying for college. Besides, it's so much easier keeping peace, and if you don't do what they say they might cut you off, not pay for school or worse yet, write you out of the will.

My father lived under his father's rule for many years. The problem was he could only live against his nature for so long. As an adult Dad stood up to my grandfather and he ended up losing the connection to his family and his inheritance. But giving up your life to one that is not aligned with your values and belief system is far more tragic. It breaks your soul. You will eventually resent the people controlling you, and the connection would have broken anyway.

Most often you do not have to choose between approval and your life. Give those you love a chance to see the light. Explain why you must follow your dreams, tell them who you are and what you are doing, and they just might listen. If you live a lie, or do not communicate your needs, anger fills the space and reactions tear down the barriers when the truth unfolds. By accepting control and responsibility for your life, they too must accept the challenge of allowing you to live it. If they don't, then that is something you don't have control over. Love them for loving you enough to want the best for you, but stand strong on your convictions. This is *your* life.

> *"If you don't stand for something*
> *you will fall for anything."*
> ~Malcolm X

If you are living a life of another's choice, in career and lifestyle, one that is not congruent with your values, dreams and wishes, then you are not living. Not until your desires match your values and align with your actions, will you be able to reach unlimited success. You may make a good living, feel safe, and be comfortable living the life someone created for you. If safe and secure is what you want, this might not be the book for you. *Flight to Success* is about being bold and authentic, finding yourself, and reaching *your* dreams. This is about how to deal with insecurity and finding success on the other side of that discomfort.

An equally misdirected path is one that you live opposing someone's wisdom for the sheer purpose—you can. Do you go left because someone told you to go right? If someone in your life encourages you to go one direction and you do just the opposite to spite him or her, you are a puppet of another kind. If you live a life fueled with behavior to prove you no longer have to listen to anyone, and can do whatever you want, you are not living the life you were designed to live.

For all those parents and friends trying to give guidance to someone you love, having faith in them to follow their heart doing something you do not think as wise, might be the hardest thing you will ever have to do. I believe in knowing yourself and following your dreams with all my heart, yet while in the editing phase of this book my middle daughter announced she was thinking of quitting her job. She recently became a single mom with a large mortgage and two kids to support. She needed security. *Don't quit!*

I stepped back with this epiphany, and an understanding of how hard it is to allow our little birds to find their own way. Her current job took most of her time, and she made less money than the part-time jobs she worked while trying to make ends meet. There was no personal reward in what she was doing, but it was stopping her from moving forward. She was not happy sitting in a room writing grants in an office without windows. For her to stay in that environment she would have sold her life for some sort of perceived security. But my first reaction was—get nine month's salary in the bank before you leave. Be responsible! Her father and I discussed the opinion that she stick it out while working her side jobs so she had security. Even though it didn't pay much, there was a guarantee.

There are no guarantees! I am here to tell you that a company can close down tomorrow. Seven of my eight airlines no longer exist. Your loved one can die. You could end up with a terminal disease and six months to live. You must figure out who you are and what you want, and live your life following that passion with faith that you are doing the right thing.

Here's the deal—those who quit because they don't like working, the job is not up to their standards, etc., and make a choice to sit on their butts while waiting for something better to come their way; this does not equate to success. Success comes from making the hard decisions, shaking up your life, and working toward a better life. We often have to do the crummy jobs—this is called paying your dues, to support the family, etc.—but there is a time to move on, and if you face your fears and are prepared, you can do anything.

This was the time for my middle daughter to move on. She is educated (about to defend her dissertation), talented (illustrates children's books and designs covers) and is not afraid to work. She was also paralyzed when she was 21-years old, and told she may never walk. Perhaps defying those odds helped to build the courage for her to continue to reach her dreams. Those building blocks of challenges really do provide strength.

I have complete faith that the perfect job will come to her now that she has committed to moving forward. The point of this story is that each person has a journey, and we must allow them to live it. Give advice, share your opinions, but support those who find the strength to move beyond *your* comfort zone, to live their life.

Why do you do what you do? Who are you? Figure it out and own it because this is your life. Clarity in values and behavior is essential on your journey to success. When you know who you are, you *will* know what you want and where you need to be. If you don't like the person you have become, you have the opportunity to change.

"Things do not change; we change."
                                    ~Henry David Thoreau

IF YOU FLY ONE DIRECTION AND REALIZE THE PERSON YOU HAVE BECOME IS NOT WHO YOU WANT TO BE, YOU HAVE THE POWER TO CHANGE DIRECTIONS.

AUTHOR JENNIFER LESHER built a six-figure career in the corporate world, but had always loved aviation. She also dreamed of writing a book. She took on a very personal challenge and wrote a story, *Raising John*. Shortly thereafter, at the age of 48, she quit her job and went back to school to become an airplane mechanic. Writing a book proved that anything was possible. The story she wrote gave a clear picture of life and the power of change. She figured out who she was and realized this was her chance to become that person.

We have one life, and it must be lived with passion. Do you want to start your life today or in thirty years? Anyone can change, just as Jennifer and Marc have proven. But if you have the chance to fly non-stop to your dreams by finding clarity of whom you are today—do it.

Many people don't follow their dreams because they have not found the courage to change. They feel they have invested too much time and money into a career or education to give it up. They are afraid of losing security. They believe they are too old. Or perhaps it's just easier allowing someone else to make decisions so you don't have the responsibility if it doesn't work out.

On an airplane, pilots live and die by the decisions their fellow crew members make. Thus we are taught to be assertive with respect so we don't follow another pilot into a burning hole. This is *your* life and you must become responsible to all the decisions you make. This doesn't mean *not* listening to others advice—this is about being assertive with respect. This is about finding your voice and being daring enough to live by your own conviction and accepting *your* failures along the way. Accountability is essential on your *Flight to Success*.

> *Know who you are. Own the choices you make in life.*
> *Learn from your mistakes and*
> *become a person who is accountable*
> *and accepts responsibility for your actions.*

HOW TO CHANGE YOUR LIFE

YOU DO NOT have to dump your life upside down to figure out who you are. My goal was to become an airline pilot. I found my final home with a major airline, and had the career. I was married with children and lived in a nice home. But life was not perfect, and something was missing.

My family dynamics growing up had been a challenge and knocked at the door of my current life; my daughters were teenagers, and I had some major health issues. On my days off I was also working nights in a simulator to make ends meet; financial struggles were many, and exhaustion was overwhelming. The decision to no longer live that life propelled me to find a solution. Thus I added one more thing to my plate—I returned to college. I actually used my student loans to pay the mortgage for a few months.

I began a master's in education, but the second quarter I shifted to human services, as I had more passion for what made people tick versus administration. Not only did I learn about others, I figured out my identity. This identity thing happened by chance, and my life took off from that point in a different and positive direction. Were there struggles? Yes. But shifting from living in a continued struggle, to learning how to use those challenges as lessons, solving problems, and feeling gratitude shaped my future. This all began by figuring out who I was and what I valued. I also learned that the darkest times of your life can turn into the greatest light, if you do not give up.

The challenges you face will make you stronger. They will create strength and enable you to conquer anything. Those moments develop you; they do not define you. Not being hired by United Airlines did not define my ability as a pilot. Not getting an interview with Alaska Airlines did not define my level of success. Finding a tumor in my body did not make me a victim of circumstance, but gave me another challenge to conquer. Events do not define you, your choices do. You get to decide if you want to be a victim or the successful person you were born to become.

LIFE OF CIRCUMSTANCE

YOU WERE BORN to endless possibilities—this is your birthright. Where that process began determined the type of training you received, it did not destroy your chance of success. Some of you were allowed to learn about your environment with loving support. Others were blocked from exploration with overprotective parents. Maybe you were left to fend for yourself, or lived in pain because those who were supposed to care for you hurt you instead. Someone you love left, others lied, and some may have died. You might have been given away to another family, or left in a dumpster. That part of your life is over.

THE GREATEST SUCCESSES
COME FROM THE GREATEST LIFE CHALLENGES

DESPITE YOUR BACKGROUND, the excuse that your environment determines your ability and your life outcome does not hold weight on your journey to success. Who you are today and what you want determine your flight level. Successful people have broken free from extreme poverty and others have come from wealth; one or the other does not define success.

YOUR ACTIONS,
NOT YOUR CIRCUMSTANCES, CREATE SUCCESS

CONTRARY TO YOUR circumstances, you are all in the same spot doing the exact same thing at this moment—reading this book and searching for the answer to success. What you do from here forward is your decision. Take responsibility.

This is your time to start writing the remainder of your story. Janine Shepherd was training for the winter Olympics when a truck hit her. Left for dead on the side of the road, she was bleeding out. Emergency vehicles got to her in time and saved her life. After months in the hospital, she sat in her kitchen, paralyzed, and unable to walk wondering what she would do for the remainder of her life.

Athletes define themselves by performance. Their bodies are tools of success. Janine lost the essence of the woman she had become. She lost control of the body that defined who she was. As she sat in that kitchen, in an emotional place where most people would feel their lives were over, she heard a plane fly overhead. Looking at her mother she said, "Mum, if I can't walk, I will fly."

"All discomfort comes
from suppressing your true identity."
-Bryant H. McGill

DECIDE TO FLY

YOU CAN DECIDE who you want to be, under any circumstance, and have a beautiful life. But beauty only comes when your actions are congruent with your values. As it turned out, Janine valued challenge and her new life was what she had trained for all her life. The world loves Janine and her spirit. We have followed her through life challenges and into the sky with such inspiration, and with more power than any race in the Olympics could have held. A race is over in a few minutes or a matter of seconds. Life continues.

When I began writing fiction, the question tossed about was which was more important in a novel, the characters or the story. I believe if we love the characters enough, we will follow them through *any* story. We cheer and cry for them, hoping for their success. Those we love the most are not perfect, but that's what we love about them—they are real. Be real. Allow the world to cheer for you. Before I could bring my characters to life on paper, I had to know who they were to understand how they would behave in the situations I threw them into. Their actions had to be congruent with their values. I had to know what fueled my protagonist's passion along the journey to help her reach her goals.

You are writing *your* story on this journey to success. You are the hero of this story, and you are on an incredible journey. Knowing yourself is not an option; it's a requirement. Who you are and what you value will dictate the decisions you make along the way. Values congruent with actions will determine your level of success. This has nothing to do with being perfect, but everything to do with figuring out what drives you. Embrace it and use it to your benefit.

> *"Be who you are and say what you feel*
> *because those who mind don't matter,*
> *and those who matter don't mind."*
>
> -Dr. Seuss

Success comes from being authentic in all aspects of your life. Anthony Robbins teaches a great lesson on how to find the perfect relationship. He recommends you write down all the qualities you want in the other person, and make sure they are values you live by in your life. This is about being authentic and living a life so those who are congruent with your values will join you. Be real. You can only fake it for so long.

Airlines want employees who fit their culture. For the first year in a pilot's job they are on probation—the time they can be fired for just about anything. It's difficult to fake behavior for a year, let alone a lifetime. Eventually the real person comes out. Let that person out now so you don't go through life lying to everyone and yourself. If your personality doesn't work with a company, or in a relationship, nobody wins. If who you are does not mesh with the world you are attempting to live in, change your location, or change yourself. But something must change. Align your life with your personality and success will follow.

BE YOURSELF

OCTOBER OF 1996, I stepped into a room full of dark suits. Some skirts, but the majority pants. Men wore red ties, and the women wore white shirts with attached bowties. Hesitating, I glanced at my attire—black pants, a black sports jacket over white business shirt, with a black tie covered with bright orange jack-o-lanterns. This was phase-one interview for an International Airline, and Halloween is one my favorite times of the year. Standing tall, I entered the room with a smile, and the first employee I met said, "I love your tie!" as did everyone else I spoke with. After the testing phase, I was invited back for the panel interview.

The following week, while waiting in the lobby for the phase-two interview, I sat with another pilot. "Do you want me to give you a practice interview?" I asked, in hope we could talk away the

nerves we felt. He said, "No. I know all the questions. I'm good."
He went first and I waited. I had no idea what they were going to
ask, *how did he?*

It wasn't long until the 'I'm good' guy zipped past and out the
door without eye contact. Shortly thereafter a woman came to get
me. She escorted me to the top of the stairs, stopped in the lobby
and turned toward me. "We have been getting people in here who
are answering the questions before we get them out of our mouths.
We have your resume. We already know you can fly. We know
about your flight experience and your education. We have only a
few minutes to get to know *you*."

That was the key—they wanted to know *me* and if I was a fit
for their company.

At the end of the interview they asked if there was anything
I wanted to add. *We have only a few minutes to know you*, echoed
through my brain. I took that opportunity to give them what they
wanted. I shared with them the personal aspect of my life, raising
three daughters—teenagers at the time—and life challenges that
correlated with flying.

Everything we experience in life becomes the foundation of who
we are. How we deal with the most challenging times demonstrates
our emotional stability and becomes a predictor of our ability to
handle life—and emergencies in an airplane. How we deal with
problems—life situations—indicates our ability to problem solve.
There will always be times when something occurs in a plane that
is not covered on the checklist or in a manual. Equally so, there
is no 'how to' manual for life. If I were interviewing applicants, I
would want to know my applicant could deal with the unwritten
challenges—wouldn't you?

They already knew I could fly. They wanted to know me.

By adding my unique skills to the table, I showed them that I could put on my oxygen mask and handle what life threw my way. We don't want puppets running the world. Sometimes it feels that way where operations live and die by a chain of command. But you are excelling beyond mediocrity on your journey to success. Those you lead will follow—not because they have to, but because they want to. Being the captain of your life is about leadership.

After we finished the interview, I sat in the waiting area for what felt like an hour. In actuality, within minutes my escort was standing before me. With a smile she said, "We are going to offer you the job." With a huge grin she added, "Honestly, I think it was your tie that did it." I laughed and said, "That works for me!" The tie I wore to this interview was black with dozens of pilot Snoopys and polka dots covering it. Confidence to be myself may have indicated a confidence in the cockpit too.

Clones get pretty boring
even in a world of sameness, and what will set you apart
from the others is your ability to be yourself.

In this game of life, there are times when authenticity outplays a same-suited stereotype. There is a reason that everyone wears the same outfit—they want to fit in—a sea of mediocrity. When I see someone standing out, I see uniqueness, confidence, and success. Go for the unique person you are, because you are incredible and there is nobody in the world like you. You are here for a purpose. That reason will only surface when you allow the real you to emerge.

"An independent view of how I see and perceive myself is all
that I need to become whoever and whatever I want to be."
-Eleesha,

Who are you? More importantly, who do you want to become? Define yourself. If you know yourself and what drives you and brings you joy, you can make anything happen. If you don't know—figure it out. Invent yourself. If you don't like who you are—re-invent yourself. You will grow, and sometimes into a different person than you thought you were. Make an introduction and start anew. Nothing in life stays the same, and neither will you.

Years ago, while working a freighter to Los Angeles, I read *Screenwriting for Dummies*, and told the crew that I was going to write a screenplay. The next day on our layover I met the captain for lunch in a restaurant in Beverly Hills, and we took a seat at the bar. I excused myself to use the restroom and when I returned, life gave me one of those lessons on identity. There was a beautiful blonde sitting in my seat flirting with the captain. He had that look of importance about him—he could have been a movie producer. I took the seat beside her.

The captain smiled as this woman told him about her search for stardom. When he finally could get a word in, he introduced me. She glanced my way with a quick, "Hi," and then her attention was back to him (with me at her back) telling him about her acting experience. Grinning, he nodded my way and said, "You should talk to Karlene. She's a screenplay writer." The woman flipped her head so quickly that her hair whipped him in the face and he was forgotten. I was her new best friend. All because he said that I was a screenplay writer—my new identity.

I do not profess telling people you are someone you are not. The point I'm making is that you can become anyone you want by deciding to. Work hard. Do what it takes and then go live that life. If you decide you don't enjoy the choice you made, change it and do something else. This is your one and only life—how will you live it?

Do your values match your vision? Are you doing what *you* want, or are you a victim of a puppet master? You are the hero of your story—who are you? When you know the answers to these questions, your life will find a natural course to fly. This *is* how success is achieved. If you want the success you deserve, lose the stories of what happened and stop blaming your actions on those events. You want to be the hero that breaks free, not the victim. Let go of your stories, stop blaming others, and get on with your life. Those early years may have been beyond your control, but today and the remainder of your life is your choice. It's up to you to decide how you want to live it.

Define yourself before you continue your journey. Sit quietly and figure out what drives you and brings you joy. If you don't know, make it up. If you don't like who you are—change. Figure out who you are and walk in those shoes. Decide to be the captain of your life on your journey to success.

TAKE ACTION NOW

- Write a list of your values and passions.
- Write another list of what you do daily. Compare these lists and determine if they are congruent. If your passions don't mesh with the life you are living, why not? Is this your path or are you living someone else's life?
- Draw a line through the actions that don't feed your soul and make you happy. Maybe it's time to make a change.
- Watch the movie *The Secret Life of Walter Mitty*.

During mid-morning tea at the senior center, Tom and Pete were talking about goals. Tom said, "After all these years my goals have been reduced to going to the bathroom with more ease and regularity."

Pete placed a hand on Tom's shoulder and said, "Be careful with those goals my friend. Every morning at 6, I urinate like a horse and at 7, I empty my bowels."

"That's great," Tom says. Pete shook his head. "No, my friend, it's not so good. I don't get up till 8."

CHAPTER 4

GOALS

IT'S ALL ABOUT YOUR VISION

GREAT OPPORTUNITY AWAITING LIFE SUCCESS

*"If you set goals and go after them with all the
determination you can muster, your gifts will take you
places that will amaze you."*

-Les Brown

THERE BECOMES A time during an ocean crossing where pilots reach a point when there is no turning back. This position is called an equal time point, or ETP. Despite any emergency encountered, pilots must continue toward their destination or go to an alternate—they cannot return to the departure point. This does not mean they will necessarily land at the scheduled destination, as the weather could go below minimums and the airport could close. Nevertheless, at the ETP pilots cannot return to where they started. You have reached that point on your *Flight to*

Success—there is no turning back. You cannot undo this portion of your journey. You are headed for your goal—a four-letter word for destination. This destination is your vision—a great opportunity waiting for you to breathe life into it.

ARTICULATE YOUR VISION

THERE IS A REASON kids with posters of their favorite athletes on the wall later achieve success in those sports. This daily vision becomes a road map to their future, a mental map. Successful people can see their reality. Everything that I have accomplished from writing, to tiling a floor, began as a thought. But when those thoughts shifted to visions where I could see a compelling future, that is when they became a reality.

SEE. BELIEVE. ACHIEVE.

THE ONLY DIFFERENCE in reality with your thoughts about where you have been versus where you want to be is the timing of those events—one happened in the past, the other will happen sometime in the future. My present was nothing but a thought years ago. The desire of what I wanted became my future, and then my past.

The future of what you want begins in your mind, and is as real as what happened in the past. Your mind is a powerful tool, and if you visualize with clarity, the brain cannot determine if you are actually seeing something, or thinking about it. This is how I study flying. Pilots call this armchair flying. I call it visualization.

The night prior to my initial A330 checkride I put aircraft panel posters on the bathroom wall, sat in a hot bath, and closed my eyes. I visualized each arrival, missed approach, traffic avoidance procedures, and in my mind I pushed the correct buttons and performed the correct procedures. The panels were there so if I lost the vision;

I could take a peek and go back to the visualization. Over and over I would push buttons, speak aloud the process, and practice. This process works. Increased performance is attributed to practice, and the mind's eye did not know that I wasn't really in a plane.

Creating mental maps of how you want your future to be is how you will make your dreams occur. You, too, are programing your future, and when your brain knows what you want, the answers come. Somewhat like programming your computer. Simple terms—if you see it today you can live it tomorrow. Goal attainment takes more than just seeing the future you want to become reality; however, visualization is a first and vital step toward success.

Have you created a vision? Do you know where you want to go? Do you know what you want to do with your life? This is one of the greatest challenges for many—they don't know what they want. How do you achieve something when you have no idea what that something is? And it sure doesn't help when family and friends continually ask what your plans are. When you say, "I don't know," they take that as an open door to give you *their* dreams.

> *"Your vision will become clear only when you can look into your own heart. Who looks outside, dreams; who looks inside, awakes."*
>
> ~Carl Jung

Not knowing what you want to do with your life is okay; staying in the hangar while you decide is not. You must get out into the world and live to figure it out. Life will help you find the answers if you allow it to.

1971 found me sitting on my floor playing a game called *Careers* with my girlfriends. I was only nine so I had no idea what I wanted to do with my life. Career options included becoming a librarian, teacher, nurse, model, or hostess. A hostess was a flight attendant and all my friends wanted that job. I could not land on the spot. Instead of accepting my defeat I said, "I don't want to be the hostess. I'm going to be the pilot!" My friend told me that I couldn't be a pilot because girls couldn't fly. Her dad, an airline pilot, had told her as much. We got in a huge argument—game over, I kicked everyone out of the house.

The only reason I *decided* to become a pilot was because I was told I couldn't. Setting out to prove my friend wrong, I created the goal to fly. With no idea how that was going to happen, or if I would like flying, I pressed on. That decision to become a pilot turned into a vision, and the goal manifested into reality. This all started with a choice. You have the power to choose where you want to go. Decide.

Pick a destination and fly toward it. It doesn't matter if you choose to fly to Hawaii or Florida, but you must know where you are going if you plan on getting there. Pilots don't randomly fly through the sky looking for someplace to land. Perhaps if they're lost and running low on fuel they might, but for the rest of us we know where we are going. We know where today's flight will take us the moment we step into the plane. Tomorrow's flight might not be so clear. Those trips are often left up to scheduling gods, seniority, bidding and a multitude of circumstance—similar to life. In order to reach success you must choose a destination—the vision for your life.

Some dreams come while we sleep, and there are others that grow in our hearts and are nurtured by our souls, until we make them a reality.

I have no idea where my final flight will take me. But I know where I'm going today. Life, like weather, can change quickly and force you to take a different route or land at an alternate. But pilots always start with a plan and a purpose. If you don't know exactly what you want to do, roll the dice and take a chance. How many times do we get lucky on that first roll? Depends. I was nine years old when I decided to become a pilot. If I had flown and didn't like it, I would have created another plan. The decision in itself pointed me in a direction.

During that first flight, at sixteen years old, I fell in love with flying. Someone was going to pay me to do something that I loved—I was hooked. I headed straight for the career counselor's office and asked her how to become a pilot. She said, "I don't know what to tell you. Girls can't fly in the military. Maybe you should pick another career."

There was no picking another career—that first flight captivated me. The point of this story is that I had no idea what I wanted to do with my life, as most nine-year-olds would not. Many adults don't know what they want either. But I made a choice due to an experience while playing a board game. Two key words are at play here—experience and choice.

EXPERIENCE AND CHOICE

YOUR EXPERIENCES IN life will lead the way if you allow them to. You will know when you've figured it out because you will experience passion. The clouds will part and the sun will shine on the place you'll call home. No matter how hard the challenge becomes, you smile. No matter what obstacles are thrown in your path, you see your vision on the other side and figure out how to go around or fly over the issue. You wake up every day excited to live your life.

A woman recently asked me how I kept my passion when times got challenging—starting over at eight airlines, there were many challenges. Easy answer: Passion does not go away because of challenges. Passion is what fuels the tough times and carries you through hardships. Passion does not diminish in the face of obstacles; it grows in spite of them. If you find yourself faced with a challenge and decide what you're doing is not worth the effort, you did not lose your passion, you never really had it. Find something else that drives you.

You might change your mind many times along your journey. When you experience life, you could be exposed to something that may spark a new path. This is the reason why it's imperative to learn how to deal with fear; listen and learn from your experiences, and figure out who you are. This understanding is the path to finding yourself and what you want out of life.

"A dream is your creative vision for your life in the future. You must break out of your current comfort zone and become comfortable with the unfamiliar and the unknown."
~Denis Waitley

One of my greatest gifts in life is having the ability to attend college. Some view it as means to an end or requirement to get a job. But if you embrace the essence of a university as exposure to unknown opportunities, to meet people who are working in a given field, and figure out who you are without anyone looking over your shoulder, you will find the value. If you have a chance to get away and attend school, do it—no matter how old you are. If you're searching, there is a wealth of discovery in education and the people you meet.

My youngest daughter was determined to become a fashion designer. She flew off to Chicago after high school, attended the Illinois Institute of Art and earned her degree in fashion. This school was also a four-year university. Her passion was combined with a solid education.

Pilots always have a backup plan, and so should you.

During school she realized a fashion career was not for her, but she finished her commitment. Then she put herself through graduate school to become a teacher.

You may know exactly where you are headed and what you want to do with your life, but when you arrive and realize it was not all it was cracked up to be, don't be afraid to change. The value was in the experience. Do not begrudge the money spent and time given. That part is gone. Do not give your life away to something that is not for you.

The value of learning what you don't want in life, is equally as important as learning what you do want. If you don't like where you are at, be fearless and change careers.

My middle daughter flew off to University of California Santa Barbara with a dream to become a photojournalist. During her first year, a counselor recommended she take an upper division geology class as an elective. She was also on the track and swim teams with a passion for sports. Many things transpired during her college years. The most challenging—she was paralyzed during a back surgery and told she may never walk again. Her attitude, "*Yes I will. But if I don't, I can compete in the Special Olympics.*" A change in mobility did not mean that it had to change her passion for sports. She defied that non-walking part of the equation, and she also changed majors due to that class recommendation in her first year. She now has her PhD in archaeology.

*Life might change course for numerous reasons,
but not until you know who you are and what you want,
will you be able to deal with the shift.
Know what drives you.*

There will be times you may have no idea what road to take. Be the kind of person who is bold enough to try something new—be flexible. You never know what path you were meant to take unless you experience a few walkabouts in the search for yourself. Those paths are the fun part of life. Make a plan for your life but don't fall in love with the plan for the sake of having a plan. Take the experience of pilots who are willing to change course as necessary to reach their destination. As they say, "If you see a fork in the road, pick it up."

There will be other times when fate crashes down, telling you what you cannot do. Whether it's fate, family, or friends—the choice is still yours. Are you the kind of person who gives up, or will you stand up and start walking despite not being able to feel your legs and someone telling you to be realistic? Do you have a compelling vision that will get you out of that chair?

*You may be traveling through life with a passion for living
and something pops up on your radar that needs fixing.
Will you avoid and go another direction, or will you get
involved and create a vision of what could be
and work passionately toward it?*

My eldest daughter moved her family to a better area to raise her children. Once there, she realized the school did not have a PTA and inspiration struck. Despite the many obstacles of working full-time while raising a family and the potential lack of community support, she formed a Parent Teacher Association. What gave her the courage to take on this huge endeavor was a vision of what could be. She knew herself and her leadership abilities, and has an overwhelming belief in possibility.

There will be times in your life when you see something is not right—those are moments when it's time to get involved. Will you take the challenge despite the hard work and people telling you it's impossible? Will you see a vision for something that could be? Being flexible, flowing with life, and creating a vision is not a one-time event. This is the lifelong process toward success. The truly successful people never stop growing, reaching and dreaming. When they reach one level, they create another vision and set another goal.

Experience will shape the person you are destined to become. But the choice is still yours as to how you interpret those experiences and where you allow them to take you. Life does not stay the same, and neither will you. You are born being one person and will evolve and develop along the way. So will your life choices for a career and happiness.

Visions and goals come from many sources, but those sources are buried somewhere in the life experience. Maybe on your bedroom floor playing a game, maybe a class you had not planned on taking, maybe a realization that your passion is to give back and teach versus fame and money, maybe it was a need for a service—inspiration is everywhere.

If you don't know what career you want, pick something and head towards it. Allow the magic of life to unfold. You never know where inspiration will come from, but I assure you it will come when you are flying towards something with passion.

> *"Throughout the centuries there were men*
> *who took first steps, down new roads,*
> *armed with nothing but their own vision."*
> -Ayn Rand

TAKE ACTION NOW

- If you knew you could not fail, what would you do with your life? Write a list.
- Compare that list with your values list. Does anything match up?
- Pick a destination. Decide what fuels your passion and do one thing toward making that a reality.
- Watch the movie, *Jersey Boys*. Pay attention to where the inspiration for the song "Big Girls Don't Cry" came from. Inspiration is everywhere. Become aware and open to the magic of finding a goal.

*When you fly toward a dream
embraced by passion in your soul,
the clouds part, the sun shines, and
the rainbow guides you to
your deepest desires.*

Two friends were enjoying an outdoor lunch and noticed a public truck filled with trees, parked across the street. Two workers got out of the truck. One of the workers dug a hole, then moved several feet and began to dig another. The second worker waited a few minutes then filled in the first hole, moved a few feet and filled in the second. The friends observed this process for a while until their curiosity got the best of them.

They crossed the street and asked, "Why are you digging holes and filling them back in?" One of the workers replied, "We're planting trees." The friends looked at each other, then back at the truck. "But the trees are still in your truck." The worker who had been filling in the holes glanced at the truck and said, "Yeah, I suppose they are." He rubbed his chin for a moment, then added, "Pat normally puts the trees in the holes, but he's sick today."

CHAPTER 5

HABIT

"We are what we repeatedly do.
Excellence, then, is not an act, but a habit."
~Aristotle

THE POWER OF HABIT

HOW DOES A person write novels, exercise daily, work a full-time job flying around the world, make time for grandkids, attend a PhD program, and build a golf course in their backyard? My secret is nothing other than establishing routines and turning those routines into habits. Habits are easy—once you create the routine, the pattern works into your brain and sticks whether you want it there or not. Somewhat like programming your flight management computer—the information is in there and the plane knows where to go.

Your goal is to program your brain to help you get on the right path and make your journey easier, not more challenging. Through the power of habit you can program your life. Creating positive habits is a powerful tool. Prior to reading a *New York Times* bestseller, *The Power of Habit,* I thought achievement was from time management, commitment, and follow through. To an extent it is, but there is so much more.

When I decided to write a novel, I woke up every day, sat at the computer and wrote. Sometimes my eyes opened at 3 a.m. and I would begin thinking about the project, roll out of bed and get to work. I exercise daily because if I skip one day, the next would be easy to miss, as well. I learned to fly by visualizing procedures, over and over again. I thought about them. Not sporadically, but consistently.

CONSISTENT ACTION

Everything I do toward any goal has been accomplished by the act of taking consistent action. I built routines. Once a routine was established, that information was stored in the basal ganglia portion of my brain (you have one, too) and it became a habit. Once this inner part of my brain joined the *go-team,* I no longer had to convince myself to get moving—I had the subconscious support system pushing me in whatever direction I chose. The power of habit can be yours. All you have to do is decide and take *consistent* action. Once you become aware of how easy creating habits is, you have the power to control your life.

Pilots are trained to run the same procedures each time they fly. We call them standard operating procedures (SOPs). SOPs play a key role to ensure everyone is on the same page. Knowing what the other pilot is expected to do is essential. When a pilot does not perform per expectation, the other pilot can identify the problem before it becomes one. However, establishing SOPs is more than creating expectations for others—doing the same thing every time creates habits. By performing the same routine, we are locking behavior into our brain. When an emergency occurs taking us outside the norm, we don't have to think about standard operations and we can use our extra brainpower to deal with the emergency.

Habits are equally as powerful in the context of everyday life as they are in an airplane. They can either be good or bad, and will direct your life down one path or another. When you create a routine and the behavior shifts into a habit, you no longer have to think about what you're doing, you just do it. You don't lie in bed thinking about how warm your bed is, creating excuse after excuse as to why you don't want to get up. Unless laying in bed has become your habit, you roll out of bed and get moving. Life gets into a flow.

There are many good habits—drinking water, exercising daily, meditation, or eating healthy, etc., but equally so, there are bad habits—smoking, eating junk food, procrastination, dishonesty, etc. The great thing is we get to choose which habits we want to establish in our lives. Are you getting the big picture on your *Flight to Success*—life is about choice, and you own that choice.

> *"Ninety-nine percent of the failures come from people who have the habit of making excuses."*
> ~George Washington Carver

Research shows the best way to help a person sleep is to create a bedtime routine. Every parent that has created a successful sleep habit for their children knows that the bath, story, teeth brushing, etc., works to put them to sleep. It works because this routine created a habit pattern. The child's brain becomes programmed that it's time to sleep after the process. The sleep comes with the routine, more so than the time of night. Adults having a difficult time sleeping can create a similar routine. There was a time that I laid in bed for hours unable to sleep. Now I take a hot bath with a good book, and I can fall asleep within minutes of hitting the sheets because I trained my body with the routine.

BUILD A ROUTINE AND CREATE POSITIVE HABITS

PAY ATTENTION TO what you do daily. Has your cup of coffee turned into more of a comfort through habit, than a need to wake up? Perhaps you don't need that extra stimulation, but your brain got used to having it. What about smokers? Obviously that's a horrible routine to get into. And while we all know that nicotine is addictive, the habit of smoking itself is equally as powerful. Another negative habit that will destroy any chance of success is procrastination. I make myself take action the moment my mind thinks I can do it later. If you want to achieve success, you must eliminate the procrastination habit.

Habits can be changed. All you have to do is find the triggering event for your habit and change the trigger. Adding school to my life while trying to finish this book, I had to change my morning routine. Email and morning coffee had turned into a habit, and a time sucker. Hundreds of emails ended up lasting hours because people would respond to my response.

My morning triggering event was coffee. I needed to create a different routine. Thus, instead of that cup of coffee and computer first thing, I rolled into doing a 20-minute meditation, or went directly to the gym. Then I began working on whatever project was on my list. Email came later. By shifting that morning routine, I was able to add more to my life and free up valuable time.

If you notice, most weight-loss programs, or meditation series have a 21-day plan—that's how long it takes to create a new habit. Like everything else, you must decide what you want and don't want in your life, and then take consistent action. That action will become a way of life through your routine and habit patterns.

On your *Flight to Success*, decide how to configure your plane for the journey. Create your own standard operating procedures that work for your life and will propel you forward. You must figure out what habits you want to create, and do them. Change the others.

One of the most important habits to establish is the habit of laughing. Find humor in your life, for your health and survival during this journey. Humor is so important that this chapter was originally about humor. But then, making humor a habit is a powerful tool.

HUMOR: LAUGH LOUD. LAUGH HARD.
LIFE IS TOO SHORT TO DO OTHERWISE

BRANIFF AIRLINES HAD recently shut down and I was on the street with a few thousand other pilots. But an opportunity arrived— an instructing job at America West Airlines. To most, this would have been construed as anything other than an opportunity, but a painful life sentence. The job did not pay well and there was no seniority. I would be locked into the training department for two years and train hundreds of new-hire pilots who would be senior to me. Despite the negative aspects, this was an opportunity to learn new skills and hold a schedule that would work well while my daughters were young.

Sitting at a large table with the manager of training and three senior check airmen, the scrutiny and pressure were on. I needed and wanted this job. Competition was tough on the flying circuit and most recently I had been a flight engineer for Braniff, and was not building flight hours.

A check airman said more than once, what "a sweet young thing" I was, and the line of questioning focused on whether I could handle the most difficult pilots, having never been on America West's flight line. Their concern was if I could handle the job, not necessarily do the job. I had a B737 type rating and experience flying the line with Evergreen and Braniff in a B727, but no experience at America West or simulator instruction experience.

When asked, "Do you have any teaching experience?" I scanned the table, looking each manager in the eye. I smiled, and replied to the pilot who asked that question, "No. Not really. But I have three small children and two Newfoundland puppies. The way I see it, if I can teach children and animals, I should have no problem with pilots." That brought a great laugh and my new job.

What I knew about this group was they were all retired airline pilots. I also knew that pilots have a great sense of humor. That humor began as a survival mechanism flying in the most challenging conditions, and ultimately became a habit. Humor is a positive habit that I highly recommend on your journey.

> *"Humor is mankind's greatest blessing."*
> ~Mark Twain

Pilots joke to survive. The best captain assesses his crewmembers' demeanor and knows when to break the tension in order to keep the crew on task. Laughter reduces stress and improves performance. Anyone can feel stress in everyday life with demands at school, work, home, and uncertainty with careers. I feel stress with the overload of social media crashing down upon me. Friends on Twitter can tweet me at any time of the day or night. Hundreds of emails sneak into my inbox nightly. You can imagine the stress in an already overloaded life. Don't get me started on the password dilemma.

Welcome to life. And with life, stress increases.

"The truth is that stress doesn't come from
your boss, your kids, your spouse, traffic jams,
health challenges, or other circumstances.
It comes from your thoughts about these circumstances."
                                          ~Andrew Bernstein

The more complex life becomes with information overload, automation, technology, and procedures, the more challenging life will become. However, stress is not a result of how busy your life is. Stress is a result of how you internalize the demands. The more successful you become, potential stressors will grow in an equal or greater proportion. But they do not have to manifest into stressed feelings. There will be deadlines, tests, interviews, checkrides, obligations, commitments, and relationships, but you can accomplish them with grace if you follow a few simple guidelines for dealing with stress—do not catastrophize, laugh often, create positive habits, and live a healthy lifestyle.

Optimal health is essential on your journey. Eating right, hydrating and exercising will help maintain balance on your journey. But the best answer to dealing with stress is to find humor in your daily challenges.

LIGHTEN UP YOUR LIFE

"Good humor is a tonic for mind and body.
It is the best antidote for anxiety and depression.
It is a business asset. It attracts and keeps friends.
It lightens human burdens.
It is the direct route to serenity and contentment."
                                          ~Grenville Kleiser

YOU WILL FEEL pressure during your fast paced journey, and you must learn how to de-stress, or your health will suffer. If you are a drama queen—let it go. Stop complaining. Get on with what needs to be done and stop trying to control the Universe by thinking that you have control over others. Today is the time to lighten up. Your job is to manage the stress you have today, so it won't interfere with your level of success tomorrow.

My overloaded schedule and self-imposed busy life had been creating a level of frustration. Self-induced, of course, but all our over-loaded issues are usually our own making. However, people did not understand that sending me five emails a day, or asking me to help with a project while I had six of my own on the table was overloading.

I do not want to be frustrated by people I meet or by my busy schedule, so I purchased a book, *The Untethered Soul*. It's amazing what awareness can do for our ability to deal with most anything. This book was a bit "out-there", but there were some valid techniques on how to deal with life. One of my beliefs was in direct alignment with the author's—happiness is a choice. Most of us believe this until something really bad happens that's not our fault and we have the right to be miserable—the car broke down, or worse yet, someone we loved died. While reading this book, I decided that I would *consciously* be happy no matter what happened. Then I read that a test would come—*I don't need another life test!* Whether we want them or not, they are always there.

That same night, having just returned from a 12-hour flight with a not so happy captain, I was experiencing some serious jetlag. After dealing with the *just got home* life, I went to bed and had been asleep for a couple hours when the phone rang. 11:49 p.m. *Oh God, my test has arrived.* My first thought was who died? Nobody. Someone in India was worried about my Windows operating system. Man oh man was I upset, and he knew it. I proceeded to fail the, *be happy under any circumstance* test.

The following morning I forgave myself for failing my test and wandered into the bathroom and opened my shower kit. Shampoo had leaked over everything and was now morphing into hardened goo. I smiled thinking—*test two.* This one was easy to pass after the sleep test. Then I opened my makeup bag and makeup had leaked. At this point I laughed—test three passed. Both these events a week prior would have made me furious because I don't have time to clean up unexpected messes. But sometimes life is a mess and we cannot allow those events to control our attitude.

We can all find something to laugh about, even under the most stressful circumstances. It's not the big stuff that gets us, it's usually the little things that pile up and throw us over the edge. If you learn how to deal with the irritating nuances of life, and make laughter a habit, you will be able to handle the "biggies" with grace.

> *"A person without a sense of humor*
> *is like a wagon without springs.*
> *It's jolted by every pebble on the road."*
> ~Henry Ward Beecher

LEARN TO LAUGH AT YOURSELF

MOST PEOPLE HAVE a difficult time laughing at the funny things they do because, quite honestly, they are embarrassing. But once you gain confidence in yourself and realize that none of the little stuff really matters, you shift from worrying about what people will think, to laughing with them. When you can do that, you have hit another milestone. In hindsight we can all look back and laugh at the moments that embarrassed us. The trick is to learn how to laugh in present time.

Allow stress to dissipate with a smile and realization that nobody (including you) is perfect. If you can do that, your confidence will grow ten-fold. Confidence is one of the greatest tailwinds during your *Flight to Success*. Enable the stupid things you do to roll off your back. Have confidence that we have all been in your shoes, because we have.

One weekend I flew to Bend, Oregon, to see the grandkids. I wore a dress-shirt and blazer. I planned on wearing the same clothes on my return. When I arrived, I pulled my shirt off over my head, not bothering to unbutton it. I hung my clothes in the closet, and two days later I found them waiting for me to climb into for the one-hour flight home. Running late, I changed quickly. I pulled my shirt on and slipped into my pants, and pulled on my blazer.

I rushed to the airport and through security—jacket, shoes and purse through the scanner. I received a few smiles that I returned. I was hot, and didn't bother putting my jacket back on until I returned to Seattle. Not until I returned home did I realize that I was wearing my shirt inside out. I could not go back and undo the situation, and I'm sure I gave a great story to the other passengers to tell their families. I laughed.

I have also worn unmatched socks, mismatched shoes—one black and the other blue, told a joke and forgot the punch line, had something in my teeth, lost my sunglasses on the top of my head, and had a pair of bunny ears and tail along with a stuffed rabbit fall out of my suitcase in front of everyone during a security gate check while in uniform at Easter time.

Your choice as you experience life is whether you bitch and moan, complain, laugh, or cry—I choose laughter.

*"A well-developed sense of humor is
the pole that adds balance to your steps
as you walk the tightrope of life."*
~William Arthur Ward

There is a reason that comedy is a billion dollar industry. Laughter makes us feel good. It reduces stress and anxiety, lowers blood pressure, can improve the memory and create alertness and creativity. If you have a choice, why wouldn't you choose the brighter side? If you can't change it, laugh about it.

To do your best, you must BE your best

Health benefits of laughter are powerful, but so are eating right and exercising. I touched briefly on the power of exercise, but now it's time for the lecture for those who say, "I don't have time." You don't have time not to. Creating a habit of good health will carry you far and enable you to live a quality life and be around to enjoy your success at the end of the day.

High achievers are the busiest people I know. They also have health at the top of their priority list. There is a reason we put on our oxygen masks before helping others—you're no good to anyone if you're dead. You also can't perform your best if you're unconscious.

A mission-driven life—shooting for the ultimate success—will reduce the amount of time you have for yourself and induce stress; all the more reason you must make time. The sooner you create a routine for optimal health, the better off you will be. I read while at the gym; I do leg lifts while watching the news. My husband and I talk while taking a walk instead of sitting on the couch. There is time for your health and you must make it a priority as if your life depends upon it, because it does.

Healthy eating is also important on your *Flight to Success.* We are growing a generation of drive-thru fast food junkies, thinking that we're saving time on the rush through the parking lot and eating in the car. Restaurant eating is an oxymoron to good health, and if you're going to be successful you must practice making good choices for your body. Most pilots make health a top priority. Not only are we required to have a physical twice a year, but the stress on our bodies flying across time zones, dehydration and sleep challenges are detrimental.

I exercise daily and eat the best I can. There are times I don't have the best choices available, but I try. One day on a layover in Paris, I realized that my routine of exercising first thing in the morning and then getting ready for my flight meant that the first time I would eat would be on the plane ten hours after being awake, which also meant I would go 20 hours without food. This was a bad habit that needed to change.

My youngest daughter had become a fitness and nutrition coach and she introduced me to a nutrition drink that her clients used. When I read the ingredients, I saw how many nutrients were included and knew this is what I needed. Now I make that my daily routine on the road. Dump a pack into a bottle of water and that drink gives me the necessary nutrition until the next meal. There is a way around any challenge. Find what works for you and do it.

PAY ATTENTION TO SIGNS—THEY HAVE A PURPOSE

ANDREW HARTLEY HAD been previously diagnosed with hypothyroidism, but the condition was managed with medication and he maintained a first class medical certificate. His prescription had been the same for years, so he failed to see a doctor in over a year for a checkup. However, two weeks prior to his Aviation Medical

Examiner (AME) appointment he visited his family doctor and blood was drawn. They noted his prescription required an adjustment. Unfortunately Andrew did not listen to the message and took no action. He also allowed his medical certificate to expire, as he procrastinated taking the examination.

Andrew never believed that this situation could be a problem—denial is a river heading to disaster. When Andrew finally visited his AME, he lost his medical certificate. He is (was) a professional flight instructor and his livelihood was gone.

On your journey, your health can be taken in an instant by unforeseen accidents. But many situations you have control over. Make your health a priority and pay attention to the signs. Be proactive. A habit of ignoring your health is one that must be changed.

Habits turn into security blankets that end up controlling your life. If you're already stuck with habits you don't want, change them. It's about changing your routine. Build positive habits by creating a routine of health, laughter, and discipline—you will be that much closer to your destination of success.

TAKE ACTION NOW

- Evaluate your life. Replace dysfunctional habits with something positive.
- Choose one thing that could make your life spectacular and do it religiously for 21 days—then for a lifetime.
- Read the Power of Habit by Charles Duhigg
- When an unwelcome emotion of anger or frustration finds its way under your skin, take a step back emotionally, look at the situation with an outside perspective, and find something humorous to say.

- When you do something stupid, laugh at yourself and allow others to laugh with you.
- Create an exercise routine that you will do every day.
- Pay attention to what you eat. Pick one food that's not good for you, and make a decision to give it up for a month. Learn how easy it is to control your cravings.
- Go to a funny movie this week and laugh.

Habits create the tapestry of life
in the fabric of existence.
They will either lift you high
or hold you down.
The choice of which, is yours.

Tom was walking down the street and noticed his good friend Pat standing nearby with a very frustrated look. Tom approached his friend to ask what the problem was. Pat replied, "I am so frustrated with the people of this city!" Tom asked why, and Pat responded, "I've been here for several hours, and have asked a dozen people what time it is, and they all gave me a different answer!"

CHAPTER 6

TIME

TIME: THE ONE THING WE WANT THE MOST, HAVE THE LEAST OF, AND WASTE MORE OFTEN THAN ANYTHING ELSE

"Time is free, but it's priceless.
You can't own it, but you can use it.
You can't keep it, but you can spend it.
Once you've lost it you can never get it back."
~Harvey MacKay

AN INTERNATIONAL AIRLINE B747 second officer had stayed in his position for fifteen years awaiting an upgrade to first officer. His seat as a second officer was between and directly behind the pilots' seats, providing the best observational view. While he had specific duties on his systems panel, an important portion of his job was to be the backup set of eyes for all that might go wrong up front. The difference between a flight engineer (FE) and a second officer (SO) is that the SO is also a pilot, and an FE is a mechanic and not require to hold a pilot's license. The person in this story was a pilot.

For 15 years, at 80 hours per month, this individual sat in that seat and flew around the world with multiple departures and arrivals. I'll take the liberty to knock off 2,400 hours for vacation, sick leave, and a strike or two. Nevertheless he was in that cockpit for, more or less, up to 12,000 hours throughout his career.

One day his seniority number came up, and his dream was about to come true. He was going to become a Boeing 747 first officer, and off to school he went. Unfortunately, after a month of training his performance was substandard and he failed his initial checkout. The training department gave him additional simulator sessions to get him up to speed. The added training did not help. When he was told he would not upgrade, but return to his old position, he argued that it wasn't fair. He demanded more time. The company had already heavily invested in this student, and the instructors felt compassion for him, so they gave in. He received another simulator session, but his performance was still below par, and he did not pass his check. This time all parties involved went to a training review board meeting to discuss the situation.

During this meeting one of the instructors finally said, "We have done everything possible to help you through this program. What more do you think we could have possibly done?"

This pilot said, "Well, you could have given me some observation flights."

APPRECIATE EVERY MOMENT

*"Waste your money and you're
only out of money, but waste your time
and you've lost a part of your life."*
-Michael LeBoeuf

THE GREATEST PROBLEM with time is that most people don't appreciate it for what it is, and they certainly are not using it wisely. Instead, time wasters manipulate and blame the lack of time for their failures. Pay attention to those who talk about time, and you will hear the excuses—it's moving too fast, not fast enough, or the most common—they never have enough of it. The truth is that most people don't respect time. They have enough to achieve their goals but they not only don't use it judiciously, they waste it.

What could have been more important for that B747 SO than to use his time in the second officer seat than to pay attention to what the pilots did on each leg of their flight, and use that time to his advantage? They were paying him to be there, he had opportunity, so why didn't he pay attention?

Time is the *only* thing we all have in common. Everyone has exactly 7 days in a week, 24 hours in a day, 60 minutes in an hour, and 60 seconds in a minute. The difference between successful people and those who never reach their dreams has either to do with poor time management skills, or the excuses they make. *I don't have time. I wish I had the time. I'll do it tomorrow. If only I had time. Someday I'll go back to school. Someday I'll take flying lessons. Someday I'll visit my friend. Someday I'll write a book.*

When you say, *I don't have time,* you are lying to yourself. If you waste today, you are misusing the most precious commodity you own. When you say, "*I'll do it tomorrow,*" you have boarded a flight in a direction opposite to success. That flight to *someday* is headed to an airport called nowhere. This is a place where tomorrow *never* arrives, and everyone on this flight carries a lot of baggage—the stories they tell of *why* they don't have time. If you want to achieve success, get off that flight!

You are reading this book because you have chosen to be on a *Flight to Success*. Lose the baggage—those excuses you make as to why you are not successful. Stop manipulating time, stop lying about the lack of it, and stop blaming time because you are not willing to use it as the gift it is. Time is yours. Believe it, use it discerningly, and change your language from, "I don't have time," to "I'll make time." Change your language. Awareness and the smallest shifts can make the greatest difference.

> *"The future is something which everyone reaches at the rate of 60 minutes an hour, whatever he does, whoever he is."*
> ~C. S. Lewis

TIME MANAGEMENT

THERE WAS A time when I was the queen of "To Do" lists until my middle daughter told me that making a list was a form of procrastination. What an eye opener that was. I would spend an hour at night writing out all I had to do the following day. Time waster. Today I don't make lists unless I'm going to the store and working with an overloaded memory. Of course we have schedules to keep, and writing down appointments is essential. But listing all I had to do was a time-suck of a valuable commodity that I could have used elsewhere.

Today I write events with times on a calendar, but that's it. No daily list for me, as I have confidence that I will accomplish everything I want to do in a given day. By stopping time manipulation and scrapping those to-do lists, you will find extra time in your day. The key is doing the work instead of writing or talking about it. Spend the time you have wisely.

My greatest challenge in the time management department was an overload of Internet communications that were bombarding my life. So when a friend stopped by for a quick visit and thanked me for not dropping her off the friend list because she was so busy and never emailed, I said, "Are you kidding? You are my favorite kind of friend because you *don't* email me." We laughed, hugged, and I haven't talked to her for many months, but I know she's busy and when time permits we will connect and never miss a beat.

Blaming email for my time-sucking problem might not be fair, as email was tied to all social media. My morning cup of coffee was a triggering event that enabled me to read my email, scan Facebook, check my work schedule, and chat on Twitter, while listening to the news. This was my *light and easy* way to merge into the day. The problem was by the time I made it through all those emails, and clicked through social media, many people had already responded. Tweeters wanted to talk. I found myself wasting my day with accomplishing nothing toward my goal. I became frustrated and felt stressed because I had so much to do and no time. The time was there, I was just using it inappropriately.

PRIORITIES

DECIDE WHAT YOUR priorities are and focus your attention there. In *Awaken the Giant Within*, Anthony Robbins dedicated an entire chapter to dealing with time. We are not alone in the stress department due to feelings over a lack of time. But the lack of time is not the reason for our stress. Frustration comes when we spend our time taking care of daily demands, instead of spending time on what is really important to us.

I recently had an opportunity to attend Oprah's 'The Life You Want Weekend,' and she gave us a great exercise of drawing a circle and slicing our pie into pieces of our life. The size of each slice of pie reflected where we gave our time, in different aspects of our life, and then we had to determine if we were happy and successful attributing that amount of time to each segment of our life. This was a great exercise in time management and life value.

The question is not about giving too much time to one area, but whether or not the time spent is moving you forward and bringing you joy. I could spend 24-hours a day writing a chapter for a novel, and feel great. Or I could spend 8 hours dealing with emails and feel like I've accomplished nothing, frustrated, and anguished. The action between both activities was physically the same—sitting at a computer and writing. But one activity was creative, working toward accomplishing a goal I had a passion for, while the other behavior was more like cleaning a house that grew filthier the longer I worked at it.

Time flies while you're having fun in the zone, but crawls at a snail's pace when doing activities that do not feed your soul. While we cannot go through life ignoring our responsibilities and demands, we can learn to manage the time we have, in order to do what we love and move toward our goals. The time management solution lies in identifying and removing your personal time wasters. It also means figuring out a system that works for you.

My oldest daughter told her friends that she doesn't do email, because on her work address she receives hundreds of them and did not need more. If friends want a response they send a text. Now she has eliminated personal emails from her busy schedule. Create a system that will work for your life. Identify dysfunctional behavior and change it. I changed my pattern to work first and play later. Note: my work—writing and school—fuels my passion. Play time is my waste time.

Rearranging my day and responding to email and social media at the end of the day provided me the opportunity to accomplish what I wanted to do toward my goal early in the morning when I do my best writing.

Part of creating plans is to understand that they are a work in progress. My doing email at the end of the day has shifted into a quick look in the morning to see if anything pressing is sitting in my inbox. If there is something that needs to be addressed, I will do it at that time, everything else happens later. By changing the pattern of coffee and email, to meditating then writing created a balanced, stress-free, day filled with success. Each day builds upon the last.

Where are you mismanaging your time? Once you figure that out, you will increase your productivity. Through awareness you will find the answers and have the power to find more time in your life.

"Until you value yourself, you won't value your time.
Until you value your time, you will not do anything with it."
-M. Scott Peck

TIME-SUCKERS

WE ALL HAVE friends who call to vent their hardships, tell us about what someone else is doing, or worse—spend an hour telling us how busy they are. These time-sucking calls are the most challenging because we care about friends and want to feel empathy. When I get those calls, if I'm at a spot to break away I will get up from my desk and use that time to catch up on domestic activities. While I'm listening, I make beds, throw in a load of laundry, clean the kitchen or water the plants. I manage my *social* calls by doing those little chores around the house where I can give my attention and still be active. You also have the ability to allow phone calls to go to voice mail. Listen and respond later.

Many hours are wasted chatting about nothing. I don't mind this occasionally, and regretfully I have done that to others. Friends are important in our life and we must respect their time, and they ours. The trick is to not allow those events to take over your life because endless telephone talking is dysfunctional and contrary to success. When you surround yourself with like-minded friends who are on the same *Flight to Success* as you, these conversations and visits can be highly productive. The question is how to identify dysfunction from necessary. If the answer to any of the discussion points below is yes, then tell the person you will call them back after you finish whatever project you are working on. Your friends care about you and will understand when you cannot talk.

- Your friend is sharing the same story they told you the day or week before.
- The conversation is about someone else.
- Your friend is telling you how busy they are and all they have to do.
- Your friend calls you, but they are distracted with something else.
- Your friend is trying to convince you to do something, when you told them no.

I am not telling you to dump your friends or to blow them off. I'm telling you to create an awareness of who is taking your time, then figure out how to deal with the situation. There is a time and a place for everything, but your time is valuable. Real friends will respect that and always be there. During this journey, put yourself at the top of your priority list and see how it feels.

MULTI-TASKING CAN BE YOUR BEST FRIEND

"The only reason for time is so that
everything doesn't happen at once."
-Albert Einstein

I AM A multi-tasker and writing this statement was done on an elliptical trainer. However, there is a school of thought that says multi-tasking is inefficient because of the impossibility to do anything well when you do multiple tasks at once. Numerous aircraft accidents have been attributed to overload because pilots were bombarded with too many tasks during an emergency and missed important cues. The multi-tasking I'm talking about is the kind that does not combine events that overload your working memory to failure. This multi-tasking is about identifying what tasks can be combined to help you create more time in your life. There is no danger in watering plants while a friend tells you about her failed dinner party.

I read and exercise at the same time. I cook and talk on the phone at the same time. I plot novels during walks with my husband. I tweet while I play scrabble and he's thinking about his word. I always have a book with me in the event I'm stuck in line or have to wait at the dentist.

There are only so many hours in your life, so you must figure out how to get the most out of them. My combination of events does not interfere with each other; on the contrary, exercising while reading actually improves concentration and retention due to oxygen flow and movement.

"Time = Life, Therefore, waste your time and waste your life, or master your time and master your life."
~Alan Lakein

ON-TIME PERFORMANCE

AIRLINES ARE GRADED on on-time performance. The push to get off the gate creates a sense of urgency that is both effective and efficient. Creating a *have to do it now* attitude is the ultimate answer to time management and essential to help achieve your goals.

Have you ever had weeks to get a project done, but waited until the day prior? The final day you stressed, rushed, yet managed to accomplish whatever it was. Many term papers have been written the night before they were due. Human nature is such that when we have time, we waste time, and when the final hour arrives we do what needs to be done. Those who reach success work on their projects with last-day urgency, weeks prior to the due date.

While my husband and I helped our daughters with college and housing, they were required to work to pay daily expenses. Increasing life challenges not only created responsibility, it shrank the goof-off time and choices had to be made with limited time. The truth is, with too much time we create the habit of wasting time. Busy schedules demand time management skills be learned and adopted. The easiest skill to adopt is the *do it now* attitude. Time management skills on your *Flight to Success* will give you the greatest advantage in your life.

PATIENCE IS TIME'S BEST FRIEND

DOING IT NOW is completely different than *having it now*. Learn patience. If you have done everything you can toward your goal, then have patience and your reward will come. Focus on another goal while you wait. Read a book. Take another class. Use your time efficiently while you wait. Patience is not about delay and doing nothing. It's about giving your best, using your time wisely, and then being patient knowing success will follow.

> *"You may delay, but time will not."*
> –Benjamin Franklin

My husband and I are opposites with the *do it now* or delay philosophy. I do everything now. My husband puts it off for another day. This could be due to our nature, but it also could have something to do with our jobs. As a pilot, I have mere days, or sometimes hours, before I'm called out on a trip. I have no choice but to get everything done present time, or it might not get done at all. My husband, having an in-town job, enabled him to have tomorrow. The truth is, you might not have tomorrow.

LIVE LIFE TODAY

YOU ARE ON a journey to success so you must be as efficient as possible with the time you have. When you wake up in the morning, accomplish one thing toward your goal before you do anything else so your day begins with success. Accomplishing something toward your goal first thing in the morning, on a regular basis, sets up your life for achievement. Once you begin living the *do it now* lifestyle, you will find pockets of time to goof off. Better yet, you have created time for opportunities that will show up at the most surprising times.

IDENTIFY YOUR PRIORITIES

THIS BOOK WOULD not be in your hands if I had not changed my morning habit. The adage, eat the frog first—do the one thing you don't want to do and the rest of the day will be great—is a survival mechanism and not a route toward success. If you eat the frogs first, your life will be full of them. There will always be one demand after another that must be accomplished. Spending your entire life doing things, eating frogs, you don't want to do, will leave little time for those activities you enjoy that will lead to your success.

To reach success, the tasks you *should* accomplish first are those that you look forward to. They should be the things that are at the top of your priority list—the very things that move you toward your goals and dreams, and ignite your passion. If you take one action a day toward your goal, those tasks will compound.

SHIFT WITH THE FLOW OF LIFE

LEARN TO BE flexible and slide items on and off your plate to accommodate your schedule. Life is not static and when stuff happens, don't stress about it, dance with it. Your focus should be on what it takes to keep moving toward your goals, not fighting uncontrollable events. Take time each day to push a little bit further. Sometimes that push may be sideways.

My priority was to get this book done before school began in fall of 2014. As hard as I tried, that timeline did not happen due to unforeseen obligations that popped up over the summer. While I did not meet that schedule, and despite my PhD program in full swing, I created time to finish because I made it a priority. While I am behind a pre-planned schedule, that's okay. Flexibility is my friend. I am creating time that I did not think I would have, further proving we have time; we just need to organize it accordingly.

Another huge part of my success formula is to fill my days as full as I can make them. When you fill your life with things that bring you passion, you feel jazzed and energized. When you fill them with tasks moving toward your goals, you feel success. Unfortunately, this overload makes some people feel uncomfortable. I have friends who attempt to help me with my busy schedule by telling me that I have too much on my plate and need to empty it.

On your journey to success, prepare for a full life. Despite what others recommend, busy people do not have to dump things off their plates. Busy schedules might make others feel uncomfortable, but for us they are the fuel that keeps us flying. An overflowing life will create time constraints that push you to become more efficient, because you have to. Busy people get more done because they do not have time to waste. They also don't have to make choices of what to give up. You can do it all.

The only way to achieve the success you desire is to put whatever you want on the top of your priority list. A priority list is not a to-do list—a priority list is your chart to success. Your challenge will be juggling your priorities while designing your life for success. With a dream in sight, you can make it happen because you have motivation (and no time to delay).

"Lost wealth may be replaced by industry, lost knowledge by study, lost health by temperance or medicine, but lost time is gone forever."

-Samuel Smiles

YOU HAVE TIME. UNTIL YOU DON'T.

STORIES THAT PEOPLE create as to how their life was not a success because they didn't have time are rampant. Those people may not have time, but you do. You have time to get off that couch and create a dream, write a novel, start flying—whatever it is you want to do. Fulfilling your dreams is about shaking up your life and saying, "I *must* do this!"

Every author has heard someone say, "One day I'll write a book, but right now I just don't have the time." This is the wrong thing to say to someone who *has* written a book. Authors know that writing is one of the most challenging and time-consuming projects possible. Not until writing that book becomes a top priority for those who say *one day,* will they create time. People will continue to blame the lack of time for not meeting their goals, whatever they may be, and on the unfortunate circumstance that they have less time than you and I. If they really wanted to write a book, they would. Just as if you really want to achieve success, you will.

> *"Time is what we want most, but what we use worst."*
> ~William Penn

If you have not achieved your goal or feel lost and are floundering, ask yourself, "Why?" What's *really* stopping you? The reality is, it is not the lack of time—it's your misappropriation of the funds called time. Time is one of the most valuable commodities there is. How would you spend it if you knew there was nothing that you could *not* accomplish? Answer that question and then do it. Your level of your success will be attributed to your making time to accomplish your dreams. You have the power and the time to achieve anything—what *is* stopping you?

TIME FLIES: USE IT WISELY

> *"The trouble is, you think you have time"*
> ~Buddha

THE UNDERLYING ANSWER as to why some people create phenomenal success, while others blame the lack of time for not reaching their goals is because successful people take action toward their dreams. Successful people decide that the value of what they gain far exceeds the pain of what they experience by taking action, and giving up free time. How many hours a week do you watch television, talk on the phone, chat on social media or play video games? These are all fine activities, but are they taking you to the level of success you desire?

Unlocking the mystery of this *lack of time* syndrome is about making your dreams a must, managing your time, and taking action. Be honest with yourself and decide how you want to spend your life. Where do you waste time? Why haven't you made *you* a priority on your list? You own 24 hours a day; what will you do with them? You have time to achieve your dreams if you start today. When you learn how to manage time effectively, you can achieve anything.

> *"The best thing about the future is*
> *that it comes one day at a time."*
> –Abraham Lincoln

TAKE ACTION NOW

- List areas in your life that you waste time. Once you are aware of your personal time suckers, change your patterns.
- Get creative and find ways to multi-task.
- Create a priority list of what you want to do that will move you toward your dreams and do those things before anything else. Not a to-do-list; a PRIORITY list.
- Watch the movie, Groundhog Day. Not only will you laugh, but also you will experience total manipulation, and *max utilization*, of time even in the same day.

A doctor asked a retired airline pilot about his physical activity. The pilot explained he spent 3 days a week, and most weekends, outdoors. The Doctor asked him to tell him about it.

"Well, yesterday afternoon I took a five-hour walk, about 7 miles through some pretty rough terrain. I waded along the edge of a lake. I pushed my way through 2 miles of brambles. I climbed several rocky hills. I took a few 'leaks' behind some big trees. I ran away from a mad mother bear."

Amazed by the story, the doctor said, "You must be one amazing outdoors man!"

"No," the pilot replied, "I'm just a really bad golfer."

CHAPTER 7

TRUTH

"Honesty is the first chapter in the book of wisdom."
-Thomas Jefferson

EARLY IN MY career I commuted to work from Seattle, Washington, to Terra Haute, Indiana, via Minneapolis, Minnesota. My ride was a glamorous jumpseat in the cockpit of a B727 freighter, compliments of Express One. One night during our flight to Minneapolis, the weather was dropping rapidly below what had been forecast. We flew into the night hoping things would improve when we arrived.

Express One, a freight operator, had professional flight engineers. Part of the flight engineer's responsibility was to listen to the weather and write it down on a slip of paper and hand it to the pilots. The flight engineer listened to the airport conditions and presented great news for the crew. The weather had gone above minimums. We would see the runway about 300 feet before landing. The captain was flying and began the approach. Locked on course, the wind tossed us about as rain beat the windows making it difficult to hear in the already noisy Boeing. We were in the clouds and visibility was zero, but thankfully it was three miles at the airport, and good enough to continue. Within no time we were about to break out, see the runway, and land.

"Minimums," called the first officer.

What the...? There was no runway. The plane pressed on.

My eyes darted to the radio altimeter as we closed in on the runway, then back outside looking for pavement.

"We should've seen the runway," the captain said. His hands gripping the thrust levers to make a last minute escape—*I hoped.* A gift from the Universe gave way to runway lights that clawed through the clouds, and seconds later we were on the runway. Thrust to idle, speed brakes deployed, maximum reverse thrust, and feet pressing brake pedals to the floor, he stopped the plane. We cleared the runway and the captain said, "Boy, that was a *lot* lower than forecasted." The engineer laughed and said, "I didn't want you going to our alternate, I've got a date. I lied about the weather."

Was he serious? The truth was, the captain should have gone around when he didn't see the runway. The reality was, based on the *assumed* conditions and the stability of his approach the captain pressed on for a 'few more feet' hoping he would see a runway with the expectations from the weather report he received.

This story ended well because we lived. But the captain was angry, as he should have been. He trusted that guy sitting behind him to be honest. Not only was continuing the approach illegal, but it wasn't safe.

"Three things cannot be long hidden:
the sun, the moon, and the truth."

–Buddha

Pilots trust, but verify. We trust dispatch when they provide our routing, but we check the weather. We trust that the fuelers filled our tanks, but we still check the fuel load. Flying is an industry that we count on each other to be honest or people could die. Wondering if we receive honest feedback should be the least of our concerns—it is expected. Mistakes happen and confusion exists because we are human. But when a person lies, they tear down a system that is built upon teamwork and support. Those people are added to my list where I doubt *everything* they say. Thankfully that list is short. In an airplane, if you cannot trust the guy behind you, you will be spending your time looking over your shoulder instead of focusing on flying. This is the same in life.

As a B747 second officer instructor, one of my top priorities was to convey to my students the importance of being honest with the pilots up front. Could you imagine flying a plane where you thought the guy behind you was afraid to admit he didn't know something? What if he forgot how to manage fuel and flamed out two of your engines because he didn't want to tell you about his lack of knowledge. On the other hand, if he were honest and asked for help, a crisis could be averted. When he moved switches, you could watch and work with him.

We all want the guy who is honest, even if his ability is limited. We could trust him and feel comfortable turning our back, knowing he had our back. Experience comes from doing, and honesty keeps everyone safe during that learning curve.

EMBRACE HONESTY

EMBRACE THE HONESTY into your everyday life that a pilot expects in a plane. Live with integrity and be accountable to your screwups. We have all looked stupid at one time or another and the more comfortable you are with that, the greater success you will achieve because you are less apt to feel the need to hide your errors. It's difficult to believe anything someone says if they lie. Work at becoming that person who tells the truth no matter what. That reputation will follow you all the way to success.

On your journey you may think you are making headway by manipulating the truth, covering your ass when you make mistakes, or blaming other people for your errors. However, creating an image that you think people will like, but inconsistent with the truth, cannot last. Many promotions have resulted because of those manipulations. But whatever success you achieve early on, due to those untruths, will be short lived. The truth will catch up to you. The lack of honesty and reputation that follows will be your nemesis through life.

> *"Anyone who doesn't take truth seriously in small matters cannot be trusted in large ones either."*
> ~Albert Einstein

A captain recently said, "We all manipulate our stories to make them work." He may be right to some extent. But the problem is, when manipulation means telling one story here, and different version there, the inconsistency will be noted by those who are paying attention. Those people who pay attention will be your greatest allies for the future. Do you want your allies to know that you are a manipulator? Positive reputations are built on sincerity, and untruths chip away at your integrity.

Make a commitment to become the type of person that others can count on. Grow a positive reputation of being accountable with an attitude of honesty, and expect that of others. You don't need to create a story of what you think people want to hear—tell the truth. The story of authenticity is far more powerful than the fabricated version.

Those people who give you their fake self will eventually unravel, and their true colors will show. When that happens with someone you trusted, you will feel betrayed. Understand that your friends' need to present the image was only because they are not comfortable with who they are. They might not even know who they are because they have lived a life of being a chameleon, changing to whom they think people want them to be in order to get what they want. Learn from those people and feel empathy, then take the lesson in the value and importance of being authentic and telling the truth in your life. Friendships, working arrangements, and relationships of all kinds are destroyed because of violated trust and dishonesty. If you learn to be honest with yourself and others. Your success will explode.

TO ERR IS HUMAN

WE ALL MAKE mistakes. Nobody is perfect and errors are part of being human. But in an airplane, multiple errors can kill you. One mistake rarely leads to death; it's the combination of errors that create the perfect storm. A pilot's goal is to catch those errors before they accumulate to the point of no return. This is the essence of threat and error management. Pilots brief potential threats prior to each flight. One of those threats should never be lies, to or from the other pilots. *"Today we are facing the threats of low visibility, a wet runway, and it's late so we're all tired. Let's fly standard operating procedures and pay extra attention to the radio calls and make sure we're all on the same page. Oh… and I might lie to you on occasion if I think it will make me look better, so watch out for that too."*

Honesty does not mean you won't make errors in judgment—you will. However, by speaking the truth you will have people around you willing to support you. When you are in error, they can step in before the worst case happens. Speak the truth and when you make an error, deal with it, don't hide it.

After Braniff shut down, I heard that one of the chief pilots was at America West. I found the number and called. "Hi Billy, my name is Karlene Petitt and I worked for Braniff, based in Kansas City. I heard you were working for America West and was wondering if you could help me get a job."

He laughed. When I asked what was so funny he said, "You are the first person of my new thousand best friends who honestly told me why you were calling. Everyone else said they called to chat and see what I was up to. Let me see what I can do and I'll call you back."

He called back—but only because of the honesty. You may think you can avoid the truth, but you rarely do. I am sure you know someone who is less than honest—those people who make up stories to fit whatever is occurring at the time to fit their needs. Most of the time it's not a big deal so we allow the transgression to slide. But those are also the same people that we doubt everything they say. You do not want to become one of those people.

One of the greatest leaders I've known was a chief pilot at an International Airline. He was a pilot's pilot and used his leadership skills to instill honesty. Well aware we all made errors of judgment, if we were honest and learned—did not do it again—he stood by us.

If you screw up, accept your due punishment and put it behind you. Telling the truth to others will become easier the more you practice, but do not confuse honesty as to help, with a justification to hurt.

*"Our prime purpose in this life is to help others.
And if you can't help them, at least don't hurt them."*
-Dalai Lama

Some people take their 'honesty' to a level where it doesn't need to be. Similar to flying your plane above the max service ceiling, there is no purpose, with a high potential for harm. The reality is there are people who feel better when they can tear someone down. Breaking others along the way is not a path to a successful life; building others up is. Why would you tell a friend her hair looks bad after it's been cut? The friend most likely knows this, and she can't glue it back on. When you achieve success in your life, you may be on the receiving end of negative honesty as others try to knock you down. Don't listen to them.

BE HONEST WITH YOURSELF

BEING HONEST WITH *yourself* is equally essential on your journey to success. The lies we tell most often are those we tell ourselves. Once we've told them for so long we begin to believe them. Stop lying to yourself. One of the most universal lies of all is, "I don't have time." Yes you do! You just don't manage it properly. How about, "My dad made me get a job to buy a car." No he didn't. He just wasn't going to pay for your car. My favorite lie during a checking event was, "My instructor never told me that!" Yes he did, you weren't listening or forgot.

WHAT DO YOU WANT AND WHY?

YOU CAN WORK out all the other untruths on your own time. But today the most important truth is to know *why* you are in pursuit of this dream you have chosen. Find clarity for why you are running after your dream and be honest. If you are honest with what you want and why, you are more apt to get on the right plane. What is driving you toward your goal—Passion? Money? Fame? Happiness?

People work to put food on the table and pay their bills. But those who find careers and have it all—a life filled with unlimited passion, while paying the bills too, and having lots of free time to enjoy other aspects of their life—are the most fortunate. If you must work, why not choose a profession combined with something that you love to do? Loving your job makes going to work fun.

GLASS HALF FULL

WHY DO I love my job with the airline while others don't? This disparity in happiness is due to *expectations*, more than the job itself. The career did not live up to the person's expectations. My thoughts—keep the expectations low and you'll never be disappointed. Joking aside, there is something to be said about building up a fantasy in your mind that reality cannot match and chasing after something that will never be; it ruins the fun and you will never find enjoyment.

If you're honest with the job, and all it entails, and you pursue the career because you want it for what it is, not what you *hope it could be*, you will be happy, find fulfillment, and achieve personal reward. If you plan to marry someone with the intent to change them, with the expectation that in time the person will become more beautiful, successful, or nicer—it's not going to happen. If you plan a life with sacrifice because of what you might get later, you are selling your life to misery.

More times than not, work expectations revolve around money. A person chooses a profession they were not passionate about, but thought they would be rewarded in gold. The truth is, there is not enough money that will make you happy doing something that you don't like, or marrying someone you don't love. If you are doing what you love, the money is a sweet reward. If you sell your life for the dollar—that's a personal choice. But be honest with why you are doing it. The lack of honesty is what creates discontent and a non-congruent life. Live a life where your actions match your words. This is about being honest.

> *"It is not the creation of wealth that is wrong, but the love of money for its own sake."*
> ~Margaret Thatcher

Fair warning—with money as a goal, there will never be enough. I was flying with a Tower Air captain who said, "Many of the guys don't like me because I fly high time, and take any trips I can get."

"How long are you going to do that?" I asked.

"Until I have enough money to quit and spend time with my boys," he said.

"How much is that, exactly?" He looked my way without an answer. I added, "You know you could get hit by a car tomorrow, and have given up your life for the dollars you never spent, and time you never had with your children." That was the same day we watched TWA-800 blow up.

There will always be more money to be had. But in this game of life, when there are big players moving you around the board like a pawn, you might have minimal control of the outcome. You could be sold along with the company; put out on the street after a shutdown; lose your seniority, and have your pay cut as you merge to another airline. While there is much you do not have control over, there are a couple things you do—your attitude and how you spend your time. Choose wisely and honestly. Make a commitment to live with integrity. Be honest with others and yourself. Choose to be happy.

> *"Honesty and integrity are absolutely essential*
> *for success in life - all areas of life.*
> *The really good news is that anyone*
> *can develop both honesty and integrity."*
> —Zig Ziglar

TAKE ACTION NOW

- Make a list of excuses (lies) you tell yourself as to why you have not accomplished what you want. Stop saying them and reword them to the positive.
- Make a decision to always tell the truth.
- Watch the movie *The Invention of Lying* for your laughter quotient for the day.

Follow True North
on your journey through life.
Allow your compass to be your guide
in truth, honesty, and integrity.
Hold strong to your values,
for they will be your greatest success.

A man realized he was in dire straits. His business had gone bust and he was in serious financial trouble. He was so desperate that he decided to ask God for help. He began to pray.

"God, please help me. I've lost my business and if I don't get some money, I'm going to lose my house as well. Please let me win the lotto."

Lotto night came and somebody else won. Again the man prayed. "God, please let me win the lotto! I've lost my business, my house and now I'm going to lose my car."

Lotto night came and he still had no luck. Once again he prayed. "My God, why have you forsaken me? I've lost my business, my house and my car. My children are starving. I don't often ask for help and I have always been a good servant to you. Please just let me win the lotto this one time so I can get my life back in order."

Suddenly there was a blinding flash of light as the heavens opened and the fellow was confronted by the voice of God himself. "Hey come on now, you are going to have to meet me halfway on this. Buy a ticket!"

CHAPTER 8

OPPORTUNITY

*"We are told that talent creates its own opportunities.
But it sometimes seems that intense desire creates not only
its own opportunities but its own talents."*

-Eric Hoffer

WHAT IS AN OPPORTUNITY? HOW DO I FIND IT?
I WANT ONE!

PEOPLE EMAIL ME daily asking for money to learn how to
fly. *Does emailing a stranger and asking for money create opportunity?* I have been told how hard it is to find a flying job, but when
I suggest a change of location, many don't want to move. *Are these
people waiting for an opportunity to find them?* Granted, landing
that first job is a challenge because you can't get the job without
experience, and you can't get experience without the job. But are
those who ask for money, and others who are unwilling to throw a
backpack over their shoulder and move to the opportunities, doing
everything they can to create success? What *is* an opportunity and
how do you find it?

Opportunity is a gift we give ourselves by facing fear, taking chances, following our hearts, giving more than we take and above all—being prepared.

There is no doubt that opportunity can drop into your lap. A *National Geographic* photographer could live in the wilderness for months and never get the perfect shot, while someone on vacation could be in the right spot at the right moment and take the photo of the century. But even those who happen to be geographically lucky must have a camera ready and know how to use it. Being prepared is essential, but then you must get out there and make life happen! If the job is not in your backyard—go to the job. If you need money—get a job, or two.

CREATE OPPORTUNITY

YEARS AGO, Jack Thompson, a Washington State University third-string quarterback was on the sidelines during a game. The first-string quarterback was coming off the field, and the second string was supposed to be going in—the clock was ticking. Jack looked right and saw that the second-string quarterback was not paying attention. Jack took the opportunity and ran in. The first-string quarterback and the coach were shocked when they saw this. With the clock in motion, there was no time to get him out and the second string in.

The coach, clearly angry, gave him the signal for a running play. But Jack knew they needed seven or eight yards for a first down. He figured he had already ruined his football career by going in on his own accord, so he might as well go out with gusto. He changed the play to a pass. They completed the pass and got first down! He was subsequently pulled off the field and the first-string quarterback went back in.

The head coach was furious and told Jack his career was over, and during half time he was to remove the uniform because he was off the team. Later when Jack sulked in the locker-room and was about to remove his uniform, the assistant coach came in and offered him the deal of a lifetime—if Jack promised not to wet his pants, they would start him in the second half of the game.

The Cougars went on to win that game and Jack Thompson, the *Throw'n Samoan*, continued on to greatness. He became the Tampa Bay Buccaneers starting quarterback and broke numerous Pac 10 and NCAA records. He is only one of two WSU football players who have had their numbers retired. His football career took off because he saw an opportunity and went for it. His decision to throw the ball was based on taking opportunity, not one of fear of what might happen. Had he completed the play the coach wanted, the outcome of the game and his life would have been different. Had he sat on the sidelines, he would never have been able to show the coach what he was capable of.

BE PREPARED AND COURAGEOUS

Opportunities will appear. But only if you are living life and are open to possibilities will you see them as such. The prepared and courageous will be able to take advantage of the phenomena most people call luck. Your goal on this journey to success is to be prepared and make yourself available for those opportunities waiting to be discovered. But you have to jump into the game.

After a career of eight airlines, I'm now with the most highly desired airline in the industry. Ask pilots searching for an airline job, and most would put my airline on the top of the list. Did I get lucky? Some would say I couldn't hold a job. Did I take advantage of opportunities presented throughout my life? Yes, and some of those opportunities sent me two steps backwards. Were there times I did not take advantage of an opportunity? A time or two, but fate intervened.

I actually decided to turn down a job at an International Airline to stay at Tower Air, until I learned I was to be furloughed. The only reason the furlough notice went out was because the chief pilot, who was on his way to New York to tell the owner of the airline he'd better not furlough this year (1996) because all the airlines were hiring, was hit by a car. He was fine, but the unexpected delay allowed the furlough to be announced. After I was hired by the International Airline, the owner and this pilot met and the furlough notice was rescinded. Having already accepted, I decided to go with the new company.

Hindsight is 20/20 and many people believe we won't know if we made the right choices, until the end of the game, if ever. However, I have learned well before that final quarter that each decision I have made has put me where I needed to be at the perfect time. How will you make the right choice? Follow your heart and enjoy your life wherever it takes you. If you do that, have confidence that you are on the perfect flight plan. Sometimes choice will be taken out of your control by fate, but then you flow with life, and know that everything works out as it should.

WHAT IF

MY HUSBAND AND I were discussing life and career paths when I said, "*What if* I took another route instead of the path I chose, and had never left Evergreen Airlines? Where would I have ended up?" He said, "If you'd never left Evergreen, you could be the CEO right now." I laughed and said, "Perhaps, but Evergreen shut down, and I would be on the street." His response, "Maybe it would still be operating if you had been running it." You have to love this man's confidence. However, what he was saying is we never know how life changes with our interaction. Outcomes will change by your presence.

You don't know how the decisions you make will impact life around you because your actions and the associated ripple effects are beyond your vision. But our involvement will change the course of life. A friend I met at one of my many airlines told me that after his military retirement he had the opportunity to go to American, Braniff, or Eastern. He wanted to raise his children in Texas, and said, "American already had 300 pilots. I couldn't see them getting much bigger," so he went to Braniff. It was my great fortune that he made that choice as I had the opportunity to meet him at America West, after Braniff's second bankruptcy.

Had he been at American, he could have been on the fateful flight that crashed in Cali Colombia. Yet, had he been on that plane, he may have created a different outcome. Lives lost could be here and impacting the world. There are many *what ifs* and *whys* we are not privileged to know. One guarantee: Life will never turn out like it's supposed to, unless we live it. On your *Flight to Success*, you must live your life to the fullest and the best you can. The rest will fall into place, as it should. Skeptical? It's time to take a detour on our *Flight to Success*.

Welcome aboard your scenic flight through a life of opportunity. Those on the right side of the aircraft will see how life paths connect and are woven into a tapestry of success. Those on the left will enjoy the serendipitous reality of connections and choice. Together we'll all enjoy the view and a great adventure and take a few flight lessons along the way.

FLIGHT LESSON ONE: Inspiration comes in many forms, but it's the life challenges that you are willing to accept that will create lift during your journey.

At nine years old I was playing the game of Careers and did not land on the spot to become a hostess. What were the odds of me spinning the wheel and not landing where I wanted, and playing this game with a girl whose father was an airline pilot who told her that girls couldn't fly? The only reason I headed toward the sky was because she told me I could not become a pilot because I was a girl. We could have been playing a different game. I could have landed on the hostess spot. I could have believed my friend. This challenge sent me on a journey.

FLIGHT LESSON TWO: What do you want? Make a decision and go find it.

I graduated college, had three babies, and was to begin my flying career within the next five to six years. But I needed to build hours first. I went to SeaTac airport to pick up applications from the local commuters. I stopped at the Coastal Airways counter.

The agent gave me an application and while I was filling it out, the owner called. She handed me the phone and he asked, "Why do you want to come work for Coastal?" I said, "So we can put San Juan Airlines out of business." He laughed then said, "I'm coming in for a flight tonight. Can you meet me?" But of course.

*"You create your opportunities
by asking for them."*

~Patty Hansen

That meeting turned into a job with Coastal where I was flying Cessna 402's part-time between Seattle and Sequim, and flying seat support with the owner's son's while they worked on their instrument ratings. This was the perfect job while raising small children. I even got a flight or two on a B727 freighter because, as it turned out, the owner was also a Braniff captain.

FLIGHT LESSON THREE: Remember to find humor in all situations. It breaks tension and builds friendships.

My pilot plan was in motion. I was building time. However, in the good ol' days there was a requirement to have a flight engineer's rating. I heard there was a training center close to my house, so I headed that way. I walked into the building and there were four men sitting in a small lobby. They stopped talking and turned my way as I entered the building. I said, "Is Bo Corby here?" One of the men said, "Yes." Everyone stared. I smiled and said, "Which one might he be?"

One of the men stood and walked toward me with a large grin. He stood next to me, about a half a foot shorter than I. Looking at the other men he said, "I like my women tall." As if we had choreographed this play, I wrapped my arm around his shoulder and pulled him into a headlock. Pulling him close I responded with, "I like my men small. That way I can keep them under control." We all had a good laugh and I met a great friend and mentor.

FLIGHT LESSON FOUR: When opportunities arrive, it's up to you to be prepared and willing to accept them, despite fear. There are people willing to help, but only if you are working toward your dream. Put in the effort and they become your support.

I signed up for flight engineer (FE) school. One night after I put the kids to bed, I headed out in the dark of night—5 blocks to the training center—to study. This particular evening Evergreen was conducting checkrides. I asked if I could observe the session.

Two nights of observations fell into a third night with a new crew and a different instructor. The only problem was the flight engineer did not show up. They were about to cancel the training event and I said, "I can work the panel for you." I didn't have a rating, but I had watched what they did the previous two nights. I could read a checklist. Why not?

The night was a success. I even got to play second officer the following night. I did not ask for pay. I did not expect anything, but felt gratitude for the opportunity to watch and participate. What a great experience—and all because I said, "I can do it."

A month after completing my flight engineer training, a manager at Evergreen Airlines called the training center to see if I had my FE ticket. A pilot had cancelled training last minute and they had an opening in class. While most of their new hire pilots had thousands of flight hours, many had difficulty in the ground school because Evergreen hired professional engineers (mechanics). But all pilots had to go through a 'nuts and bolts' flight engineer ground school prior to flight training. I had a fresh ticket. They assumed I could make it through class.

Evergreen offered me a job—pending I could fly. Thus a simulator session was scheduled. One of my greatest fears was starting a career with young children, not to mention never having flown a jet. Bo Corby spent two hours a day, over the next three days, in the simulator and taught me how to fly the B727. He gave me core skills that I have carried throughout my career, not only to fly but how to teach. He set the standards of an instructor pilot to the highest level. Bo also happened to be a captain for an International Airline.

FLIGHT LESSON FIVE: We don't always get what we want, but we always get what we need. Do the best you can, and life has a way of developing into a beautiful play.

While working for Evergreen, I was called in for an interview with United Airlines. Oh man I was psyched! This was going to be the career move of a lifetime. My dreams had all come true. At the time, United was the leader in the industry and anyone would be honored to work there. When they turned me down, I was devastated.

I allowed myself a day of devastation (maybe two on this one) and then I wrote United a letter explaining why women could be pilots *and* mothers too. We could do it all. Their response was to encourage me to reapply. I did not. By the time I received their response, I had convinced myself I did not want to go work for United. As life turned out, I am so thankful I was turned down for that job, I'm in such a better place, with a stronger company, with so many experiences and people I have met along the way that I would not sell for a higher seniority number.

FLIGHT LESSON SIX: You might think you made a mistake if the opportunity you chose did not go as planned. But each path you take leads you to another gift. Be patient to see how life unfolds while you're unwrapping the package.

After that great rejection, I continued on with Evergreen. One day the owner from Coastal Airways called and said, "You *need* to come fly for Braniff." He and two of his sons, also working for Braniff, were on a layover together, and decided that I needed to join them. But there was a B747 bid opening at Evergreen. I was torn. Two opportunities—which direction should I turn? The dream of flying passengers instead of freight was something I could not pass up. Besides, I had a lot of peer pressure from my adopted Coastal Airways family.

They opened the doors to Braniff and I walked through them. The Dallas chief pilot hired me on the spot. I don't even remember filling out an application. That job lasted short of a year due to their bankruptcy, and I was on the street.

FLIGHT LESSON SEVEN: Honesty opens more doors than it will close. What appears to be a step back, or stagnation, could also be your greatest gift, giving you skills for something bigger and better for your future. When we go full speed, sometimes we miss the gold sitting on the side of the road.

I called to get an application from America West. They had a 1500-hour requirement. I had a little over 1400 hours. I attempted to explain to the woman in human resources that I had been flying a B727, and I had about 900 hours as a second officer, too. She said it didn't matter, and recommended I rent the cheapest plane possible and fly touch-and-gos to build my time.

That's when I learned that Braniff's Kansas City chief pilot had gone to America West. When I called to ask him if he could help me get a job, he offered me a job of another kind—instructing.

When I accepted that job with America West I was locked into the training department for two years without seniority. But I gained skills and worked a schedule that was perfect with my family. My willingness to give up an opportunity to accrue seniority, to accept another position at a significant pay loss, turned into many opportunities with training in my future.

FLIGHT LESSON EIGHT: There will be situations out of your control. You might be on the good end of the deal, or you might be on the bad—and what you think is reality, might not be the case. Don't react. Take time, experience the environment and respond once you have assimilated the situation.

I loved instructing on the B737. It was not long until they type-rated me on the B757, and I was dual qualified. Two years flew by. A couple weeks before my two-year training position came to an end, when I could apply to the flight line, America West filed bankruptcy. Everyone who had been hired the same time I was and beyond, was on the street. I retained my job because they needed simulator instructors, but I was in a holding pattern.

FLIGHT LESSON NINE: The greatest challenges in life are nothing more than training for your future. They give you skills, strength, and provide leverage. But it's you who must open the door of opportunity.

The pilots I trained were on the street, I pressed on instructing. It wasn't long until I was assigned to work a B757 training contract for Guyana Airways through America West. These students presented an additional set of challenges because of their background and misdirection from our ground school instructors. I tossed the lesson plan aside and I taught them how to fly that automated plane one instrument at a time.

While working for America West, I began instructing in the simulator for another company. This company earned the contract to supply Guyana's expat pilots—those pilots that would fly the aircraft with the Guyana pilots until they became proficient. Because I worked for both companies, I was assigned the job to teach the Expats America West procedures.

America West spent a lot of Guyana Airways' money because they did not understand the added requirements for pilots not on their certificate, thus these pilots required a great deal of training in the plane. Furious at the situation, the government subsequently invited me to work directly for their company.

Talk about fear of going to unknown places. However, it had been four years with America West and the previous two years had been nothing but conducting recurrent training. The pattern was growing old, the future stagnant and I wanted to fly, grow, and expand. I headed off to Guyana. Tasks included setting up an in-house training department, writing manuals, and creating a ground school—an entire new set of skills was being developed. In addition to teaching ground school, I instructed in the simulator. We were FAA and CAA certified, and I learned many lessons from America West's failure. I wrote training programs from home, and took the opportunity to take my daughters to Guyana while I taught ground school. The simulator we used was in Minnesota.

FLIGHT LESSON TEN: Honoring obligations trumps opportunities. Sometimes these are life tests to determine your level of integrity. When you do the right thing, opportunities will still be there. Those on the other end will know you will honor them too.

The second opportunity I had given up materialized again later. While working for Guyana Airways, I commuted via New York where I had an opportunity for a full-time job to fly a B747 with Tower Air. And while I believe opportunity only comes once—I did not jump through that door—not then.

I had made a commitment to Guyana Airways. I was the only certified instructor and check airman approved to train and sign off Guyana pilots. I could not leave. Well, I could have left, but I chose not to. There were four pilots ready to begin training and the company needed them. I would not leave the airline in a bind or play with those students' lives, despite giving up seniority and flying a 747. Once my students were trained it would be time to go.

FLIGHT LESSON ELEVEN: The world is small and the connections are many. Each event and person in your past will eventually intertwine and create another opportunity. You will have many choices along the way. Make the best decisions you can but when life intervenes, taking the choice out of your hand, you were not meant to go that route—enjoy the ride on which the Universe is sending you.

While training my Guyana students, we utilized a US-based International Airline simulator. With midnight training sessions, vending machine coffee and Famous Amos cookies to stay awake, I lived at a Minnesota-based training center.

One evening in the cafeteria, prior to our session, a pilot asked me if I had applied to his airline. I had not, so the following night he brought me an application. I filled it out the best I could without my logbooks and submitted it the following morning. Years later, while working for Tower Air, Bo Corby, that captain who owned the training center in Seattle and taught me how to fly a jet and instruct, called to tell me that I needed to apply at his airline—they were hiring. I told him I had submitted an application three years prior, during the Guyana days. Unbeknownst to me, he took it upon himself to check on my application and in doing so told human resource personnel that I was flying a B747 for Tower. He called and told me they had me on file, but I had to reapply. *Sure thing. In my spare time.*

I was working full time with three kids at home. I loved my job with lots of days off in a row and when I flew, it was around the world to exotic locations. Besides, I was also going to upgrade and become a B747 captain within six months.

Shortly after that conversation, this International Airline called me for an interview, despite my neglect to update my application. After a great deal of thought, discussion, and turmoil, I decided to stay with Tower. Yes, I was giving up an opportunity in order to become a B747 captain. The day I made that decision, I learned I was about to be furloughed. Off to the interview I went. The day they offered me a job, Tower Air called and said they had decided not to furlough that year, and asked if I could return early. I told them I had accepted another offer, but could work for them the first two weeks in December, and the first two in January. I did just that, and then said good-bye to Tower and my captain seat. Tower Air shut down six months later.

FLIGHT LESSON TWELVE: Everything you do in your life builds upon your experience and reputation. These experiences will open doors and build confidence. What you might perceive as a sacrifice will become strength propelling you forward and creating more opportunities.

The first week at my new airline we bid for the aircraft we wanted to fly. We had already received our initial assignment. Mine was the right seat on the B727—the exact seat, with the same pay, I had flown with Evergreen ten years earlier. Talk about going full circle. Despite these initial assignments, a company-wide bid was open.

It was recommended to *not* bid anything other than our initial assignment because we might have to go through two checkrides during probation. Double Jeopardy. At the time, pilots could be qualified on two different types of aircraft. I went ahead and bid all the wide-body aircraft, captain and first officer positions. With one slot remaining, I added B747 Second Officer. Guess what—I received my last choice, that second officer position on the B747.

Some pilots in my class thought that wasn't fair that I had bid something else when we were recommended we shouldn't. The company did not tell us not to, they *recommended* it because they did not want to overload us during the first year with two check-rides. At this point in my career, I had four type-ratings, and had worked in multiple training departments. I did not fear a checkout.

I sailed through B747 training, having flown the plane and understood the operation. After two months on property, I was invited to become an instructor. Having instructed for America West for four years, and then for Guyana for another two, with time in type (having flown as a first officer on the B747), I was qualified. Besides, they couldn't get anyone from the flight line to come into training. They eventually typed me on the B747-200 as part of the package for writing a training program; I flew test and ferry, became a check airman, flew the line, and trained and checked in the simulator.

During my probationary year, being an instructor gave me more control of my schedule. This meant everything while managing a career and family of teenagers at home. All this came about because of a choice to go into training and sacrifice seniority so many years earlier. I also wrote training programs for my new airline because I had the experience from doing so with Guyana.

FLIGHT LESSON THIRTEEN: Sometimes it's not the amount of money you receive, but the value of the work that will help in your career. Don't be afraid to ask, you might just get it.

Years later, compliments of that 1997 bidding card, I was awarded the right seat on the B747-400 when others more senior to me had not bid it. The entire training department was waiting to see if a twelve-year B747-200 second officer could handle checking out in a glass cockpit aircraft—the modern, two person version of the earlier B747. What they didn't know was that I had been working in a simulator on my days off, teaching B737 and B757 students to help put our daughters through college. Navigation technology, systems, and operations between the Boeing 747-400 and B757 are similar, as are flight procedures.

While the pay for these side jobs was minimal, and the hours ran from midnight into the wee hours of morning on my days off, I maintained flying skills by teaching on the modern Boeing aircraft. The reward was not the minimal pay, but experience I used years later. Just prior to a merger, I zipped through training and was type-rated and flew the B747-400 for four months.

"Opportunities to find deeper powers within ourselves come when life seems most challenging."
-Joseph Campbell

FLIGHT LESSON FOURTEEN: When your world appears to fall apart, sit back, watch and listen to the messages. There might be something that you had not realized you needed to do.

Due to a change in seniority and bumped off my plane, I was once again on a ride of minimal control. I bid Seattle A330, and was awarded the last position. After 30 years of flying I was finally based at home.

Up until this point I had only flown Boeing, but fate and a merger put me on the Airbus. Through my life I gained writing experience, worked for many airlines and have an in-depth understanding behind the scenes in training, and have gone back to school and earned two master's degrees. I have come full circle once again, but this time with experience and education behind me. The next adventure has begun.

FLIGHT LESSON FIFTEEN: Know yourself so you will be a perfect match for the work you choose. Your job satisfaction depends upon it.

My original plan, when I first decided to fly airplanes and have a family, was to work for Alaska Airlines and fly domestic to be home every night. That opportunity was derailed more than once by elements outside of my control, and put me on a new path. Knowing myself as I do now, *identity meaning everything to success,* I would not have been happy flying the same plane and the same routes daily. My success is attributed to life keeping me from a path on which I did not belong on. My life and career gave me what I value—experience, education, and growth.

"The optimist sees opportunity in every danger; the pessimist sees danger in every opportunity."
~Winston Churchill

FLIGHT LESSON SIXTEEN: Tomorrow might never come. Take a Nike moment and just do it!

Having always wanted to write a book, I'd been looking at the Hawaii Writer's Conference for years. But it was so expensive and I never had time. Despite the excuses, I had planned to go—one day.

In 2008 I was off work with a hip replacement. I had time, but without working, sick leave pay was significantly less than a full schedule. How could I afford it? *I'll do it next year.* The problem with putting anything off until tomorrow is that tomorrow never comes. When you wake up, tomorrow is still a day away. The only time to capture opportunity is today.

Then that little voice said, "You have the time. This opportunity might never come again." I signed up. That seminar opened my life to another world. I learned skills, opened doors, made connections and met life-long friends. Accepting that opportunity changed my life. This was the last year before they cancelled the conference.

THE NEXT BIG ADVENTURE

OPPORTUNITIES IN LIFE create patterns and weave paths for the next big adventure. Each opportunity will come because of something you did prior. Be willing to get out there, experience the world, do something extra, push through fear, dare to dream and take those times of stagnation as a time to reflect, educate, evaluate, and prepare for the next big race.

"A wise man will make more opportunities than he finds."
~Francis Bacon

TAKE ACTION NOW

- Evaluate and reflect. Have you given up an opportunity?
- Pay attention daily to see what comes your way. What opportunity is waiting for you? Find it. Make it. Do it!
- Watch the movie: *Won't Back Down*. This inspiring film shows the power of the human spirit of a mother and a teacher who want their children to become educated. When the system failed them, they created a school—the opportunity.

Two great white sharks swimming in the ocean spied survivors of a sunken ship. "Follow me son," the father shark said, as they swam to the mass of people. "First we swim around them a few times with just the tip of our fins showing." And they did. "Well done, son! Now we swim around them a few times with all of our fins showing." And they did. "Now we eat everybody." And they did. When they were both gorged, the son asked, "Dad, why didn't we just eat them all at first? Why did we swim around and around them?" His wise father replied, "Because they taste better without the crap inside!"

CHAPTER 9

STRATEGY

LIFE STRATEGY—PLAN WELL, BE FLEXIBLE, AND YOUR SUCCESS IS LIMITLESS

"Leaders establish the vision for the future and set the strategy for getting there."

-John P. Kotter

FLIGHT PLAN YOUR LIFE

AFTER A PERSON learns how to fly a plane, the next step is the journey. The quest for adventure is to get away from the airport traffic area and out into the world, somewhat like life. Going places, seeing things, or building flight time for a career becomes one of many goals. But before pilots can depart on this journey, there is another step that must be accomplished—creating a flight plan.

A pilot is required under most circumstances to make and file a flight plan. Elements of the flight plan include Aircraft Number,

Current Location, Destination, Route, Aircraft Speed, and an Alternate. An interesting connection to the elements of a flight plan is that they parallel goal setting.

Goal setting is an effective method for reaching dreams, thus the reason people are willing to spend thousands of dollars attending workshops. Goal setting has worked for me, and it will work for you, too. The strategy of goal setting on your *Flight to Success* is to create a flight plan for your life.

LIFE FLIGHT PLAN

AIRCRAFT NUMBER—WHO ARE YOU?

PLANES HAVE A number unique to them and this number is on every flight plan. Air Traffic Control (ATC) must know what type of aircraft will be on the route, just as you must know yourself before you make the journey. Who are you? What do you want in life? What do you value? What is driving you? What is that voice in your heart telling you? What is your unique number?

The plan you are about to create will impact the remainder of your life. Make sure you are aligning your destination with your values. If you are not clear on the importance of identity, take a few minutes and read the identity chapter one more time. Identity is extremely important to your success, and a fulfilled life depends upon knowing who you are.

CURRENT LOCATION—WHERE ARE YOU?

WHAT ARE YOUR strengths and weaknesses? What resources do you have available? Take note of where you are today. Where you begin your journey with education, age, finances, support, commitment, determination and drive will impact and alter your route of flight.

Remember, the greatest challenges give you the most strength. Have clarity about where you are beginning the trip. This journey must be designed from where you are today, to get you to where you want to be tomorrow. A clear assessment will begin the foundation of your flight.

DESTINATION—WHERE ARE YOU GOING?

WHAT IS YOUR goal? Be specific. Some people run aimlessly through life. They are so busy doing and trying to be someone that they never get off the hamster wheel. At the end of life they are exhausted, have worked hard, but never reached their dreams. Why not? It could be a time management problem, but chances are they did not know where they were going. Imagine trying to graduate from college without a degree in mind.

If you do not know where you want to go, you will never get there. This is a must in flight planning your life. The essence of achieving success is to know where you are headed.

ROUTE OF FLIGHT—HOW WILL YOU REACH YOUR GOAL?

WHAT STEPS ARE required? What type of education is needed? What connections could help? How will you navigate to your dreams and desires? Pilots rarely get cleared direct to their destination. We follow waypoints that are nothing but mini goals—a series of steps leading us to our destination. Your short-term goals will be the steps that lead you to your long-term goal—your dream.

SPEED—HOW MUCH TIME IT WILL TAKE?

HOW MUCH TIME will it take to reach each waypoint along your journey? How long will it take to reach your final destination? Answering these questions will keep you on task. Time is a great measurement to determine how well you are doing on your journey. There are times when the wind is stronger than expected and pilots search for a better altitude. You might have to find a more advantageous altitude, too. Keep track of time and do not waste it or allow it to slip by.

There are situations where pilots are going too fast and need to slow down for a segment or they will overtake another airplane. If they arrive too early they have to wait for a gate. Burning more fuel to arrive early may not be worth the expense. Fast is not always the best option. Aircraft can experience high-speed stalls just as they can at low speeds. If you find yourself out of control, running too fast, you may need to slow down. Pay attention to what life is telling you and adjust accordingly. There will be other times when you are lagging behind and need your afterburners. But the only way you can manage your time is if you create a schedule.

Estimate out how long your trip should take and be accountable to that time. Evaluate and update your plan as necessary. Pay attention to the delays. Be aware of ways to gain extra speed if you are behind the plan. If you find yourself in the jet stream screaming along, enjoy the extra push. If there becomes a negative impact, modify your altitude.

ALTERNATE—BE FLEXIBLE

Is YOUR FLIGHT plan working? If not, you may need to take a different route. At times you might need to land some place other than your destination, to wait out the weather before you continue. Life happens and planes break. You are not infallible and neither are the people around you. Circumstances occur just as a surprise snowstorm falls on occasion. Always have something to work on during the times of delay. Have a backup plan and be prepared to divert to your alternate, and know that this is part of flying and the reality of life. Patience.

BE SPECIFIC WHEN YOU STATE YOUR DESTINATION.

A PRIMARY REASON people don't reach their goals is they are not specific enough. When you fly in circles, you will never reach the airport across the country. If you have a goal to get more money, I could make that a reality by giving you a quarter. Is that really what you meant? Get in the practice of being specific. What is your long-term goal—your final destination? The more specific you make this, the higher the probability you will reach your dreams.

If you take off for Europe but have not decided if you're landing in Amsterdam, Paris, Rome or London, there might be a few problems on the horizon. Your *Flight to Success* is about getting to your destination in the most efficient manner possible. You may change along the way, but you must begin in a specific direction.

If you want to be a pilot, ask what kind—airline or corporate? Do you want to fly domestic or international? Do you want to fly a Boeing 747—then flying for the Luv airline (Southwest Airlines who operate only the B737) would not help you reach your dream. This applies with every job decision you will make. Know what you want and make a plan with details to get there.

I NEED A COLLEGE DEGREE

IF YOU ARE wondering what to major in to become a pilot, choose something you have a passion for. This will be your backup plan if the flying career does not pan out the way you thought it might. The wind may shift and you may lose your medical; leave an alternate plan open. In addition, if you love what you are studying, the education will be easy while focusing on flight training.

If you have not found your passion, think about psychology. Every job you will encounter will involve people—from business, to finance, marketing, retail and managing a flight deck; you will deal with people and their personalities and you must be able to communicate with them. Management is also an excellent overall life degree—communication and leadership skills, finance, and personal management skills will be learned. Psychology and business degrees will not be lost on any career and may help you figure out who you are, and help with skills in whatever life passion you choose.

One of my greatest lessons on flight planning a career in the aviation industry is that life happens. Be prepared and willing to alter your plan or make a new one. You may make a great plan, but the airline has other plans—shutdown, merger, closing bases… etc. Rarely will you make one flight plan and that will be it. You will have a great deal of practice rewriting your flight plan for the many opportunities life has in store.

UPDATE AND MODIFY YOUR FLIGHT PLAN

IF I CREATE a flight plan on a specific route and a thunderstorm appears, I adjust my route to fly around the cells. When my plane experiences an engine failure, I divert. If the weather drops below minimums and I can't land, I go to an alternate, wait out the weather, get more fuel and try it again later. Sometimes our delays are longer than planned, not unlike life.

When my B747 was hit by lightning en route to Guam, we were stuck five days in paradise. I use the term *stuck* loosely. If you have never been to Guam, I recommend it. The point is—your journey will take different routes for many reasons. Delays will arise, and sometimes you just have to cancel the flight. Be flexible and re-write your flight plan as needed. Life changes along the way and so will you. Your greatest strength in creating a strategy is flexibility. Enjoy the down time.

Your flight plan will shift along your journey. Mine did. But I never lost sight of my destination—I just created new plans along the way. Like a painting, you will tweak and fine-tune lines and colors throughout life. My original plan was to fly for Alaska Airlines, but fate threw me into an opportunity to fly international. Knowing myself as I do now, I found my home. The B747-400 fulfilled that mission and was my favorite plane. But as time passed and life evolved, I opted for being based in Seattle versus commuting to Detroit. My life choice of flying international is still high on my priority list, thus I am flying an A330. Priorities change and so will your dreams.

Modifying your flight plan is as essential as monitoring your path along the way. Pilots who allow their planes to drift without making corrections will run out of fuel before they reach their destination.

STAY ON COURSE

SHORT-TERM GOALS (waypoints) are equally as important as long-term goals (destination) because they keep you updated on your progress. They provide little wins along the way—the encouragement that keeps your fuel tank full. Identify them and celebrate!

When my daughter was paralyzed, I posted a calendar on the wall and each day wrote some form of improvement—your big toe wiggled more than yesterday, or you stretched farther today. Something simple. After she emerged from the hospital, I told her that it was her attitude that gave her success to walk again. She said, "Not really. I could see improvement."

There is power in seeing accomplishment, no matter how small. Allow that to be a driving force in your life. It doesn't have to be a huge change. Perhaps you learned one more fact for your instrument test today. There is great power in compounding success. With each waypoint you cross, you will be that much closer to your destination. It all starts with making that flight plan for your life.

ACTIVATE YOUR FLIGHT PLAN

HOW DID I achieve my dreams? I created a flight plan to my destination of becoming a pilot, and activated it. I did not fly blindly. I had a plan. And while my plan shifted and varied along the way with family and airline bankruptcies, I still had my destination in sight. You must never lose sight of your destination. Goal setting and visualization will be the key to your success.

When I returned to school to get my Master's in Business Administration, as well as my Master's in Human Services, both programs included goal-setting workshops before we began the coursework. There was only one reason for this task—goal setting sets you up for success.

Your dream *is* all about the GOALS: Great Opportunity Awaiting Life Success, but you need a strategy. A perfect plan does nothing if it sits on your desk in all its perfection. Success comes from living the strategy you create. You must activate the plan you create by taking action.

> *Goal setting is nothing more*
> *than mapping out a plan for your life.*
> *Pilots do this before every flight—we create a flight plan,*
> *and before we fly, we activate it.*

SHARE YOUR VISION AND YOUR ROUTE

PILOTS TELL ATC what their plans are before they depart. When they are not where they should be, someone begins looking for them. This process also makes pilots accountable to the mission—if we vary from our route or change speed significantly, we must notify ATC of our change.

Tell people about your plans. Friends and family members will keep tabs on your progress and assist you in keeping on track. They will be your support team. When you get lost or drift off course, they will be at your side. Find a friend to check on your status and to help keep you accountable.

I told everyone I was going to become a pilot. From age nine to my first flight at sixteen, there were many situations that could have kept me from it. The only reason I flew was because I had told everyone I was going to be a pilot. Tell people your plans and honor them. Honor your dreams. Honor your voice. Honor yourself.

TAKE ACTION NOW

TODAY YOU WILL map out your life and create your flight plan. Start simple and pick a dream. Decide when you want to achieve it, and what route you will take. Each point on your route will become a short-term goal and you will continue the process again with each subsequent goal. Have fun and see what kind of treasure map you come up with.

- Destination: What is your goal?
- Time: I will achieve this goal by (date)
- Route: I will attain this goal with the following short-term goals

EXAMPLE:

- Dream: I will become an airline pilot
- Time: 23rd birthday
- Route: I will attain this goal with the following short-term goals:
  - Attain four-year degree
  - Earn flight ratings
  - Interview for jobs

A little secret about your short-term goals— they need to be specific also!

- Goal: Four-year degree.
- Time: Complete by 1983.
- Route: I will attain this goal with the following short-term goals:
  - Select a university and degree
  - Select the courses I will take

o   Create a schedule that will finish in the planned time frame.

You've got the idea. Now make a plan for your life. Be flexible and dream big. Once you've completed this task, take one action today toward your first short-term goal. Share your plan with your family and friends so they can help to hold you accountable.

Have fun and dream big!

Two men were walking through a jungle. All of a sudden, a tiger appeared in the distance. One of the guys took out a pair of Nikes from his bag and began putting them on. The other guy, frozen in place said, "Do you think you will run faster than the tiger with those?" His friend replied, "I don't have to run faster than the tiger, I just have to outrun you."

Chapter 10

Urgency

*"A higher rate of urgency does not imply
ever-present panic, anxiety, or fear. It means a state in
which complacency is virtually absent."*
~John P. Kotter

TWENTY-TWO YEAR OLD Rob Akers approached an Air
Force recruiter in 1991 with the intent of becoming a military pilot. Not only was he older than most everyone else taking
this first step, he had no flight time. He also held an unimpressive
2.2 GPA in a non-technical degree. The recruiter listened patiently
until Rob told him that he wanted to become a pilot. At which
time the recruiter broke into laughter. Once he regained his
composure and was able to speak, he said, "You'll *never* become
a military pilot." Exactly what Rob feared—he was too old, not
smart enough, and did not know how to fly.

Rob had two choices. He could listen to the recruiter and walk
away in defeat, or prove him wrong. The cutoff age to join the Air
Force was twenty-seven. He had less than five years to turn himself
into a qualified applicant. With no time to spare, Rob took action

and headed toward graduate school, with a plan to raise his GPA. Rob's time compression created the power of urgency. He did not have time to drift through life like he had in college. If he were going to become a pilot, he had to add thrust and build momentum.

SUCCESS BEGINS TODAY

Success depends upon where you live between complacency and urgency. Living on the side of complacency is fine if you have nowhere to go and time is unlimited. I am not diminishing anyone's life choices. However, I am telling you—time is not unlimited and you do have something you must do. You are here for a purpose, and you are reading this book to help you get there. You want more out of life. You get more by getting your butt into the race. Not tomorrow. Not next month. Now!

You must make what you want so important that you will not allow another day to pass without taking steps toward your goal. Those who achieve ultimate success do so by creating this sense of urgency. Successful people view today as the day to get a task done. Do not wait until tomorrow when you have this moment today.

How long would you sit on the side of the pool and watch a loved one flounder in the water? The moment you realized what was happening, you would take action. Imagine it's your life that is drowning. Are you willing to save yourself? Don't allow your dreams to drown. Don't waste your life by waiting for tomorrow. You can achieve anything you want, but only *if* you take action now.

MAKE YOUR VISION A MUST

MAKING DREAMS A *must* creates that sense of urgency. Without urgency people are not motivated to excel, change, or do what it takes to reach their dreams. Rob had a great time in college, but that goof-off period could have impacted the rest of his life. When he awoke and realized what he wanted to do with his life, he shifted gears. Rob accumulated a thirty-thousand dollar debt earning his commercial rating, and worked his butt off to get into school and raise his grades. He had no time to dink-around; that part of his life was over.

When you feel a sense of it *must* get done, you will do it. When urgency meets opportunity, the result becomes overwhelming success. What if you lived your life with a daily sense of urgency? Imagine what you could accomplish.

A primary reason people *don't* reach their potential is due to procrastination. I almost delayed my PhD program another year, to a time when I had more time. Reality is—I will never have more time, and neither will you. When we have time, we fill it doing something. I would be just as busy next year as I am today. When I decided to do it now, and stop procrastinating, I studied for the GRE and was accepted into graduate school.

> *"Procrastination is like a credit card:*
> *it's a lot of fun until you get the bill."*
> ~Christopher Parker

There are two kinds of people in this world—those who do, and those who procrastinate. If you were a procrastinator, you would not be reading this book. You might have bought it, but it would be sitting on your shelf unopened with plans of reading it tomorrow. Since you are reading, you are on your final segment of your *Flight to Success*. This is that portion of your flight where you *must* get to your destination before the airport closes. It's the time when you live your life like there won't be a tomorrow, because there might not be.

On July 17, 1996, TWA 800 exploded in front of my aircraft—one of the most impacting days of my life because of the messages that came with that event. We never know when our time is up. Why waste it? My friend Mark L. Berry's fiancé was on that flight. He knows how the power of a moment can change the course of life. We both learned that we don't have as much control as we think we do. That's a huge realization for pilots who are supposed to be in control.

The only control we have is to make the best of what we have, now. Living on the sidelines is not good enough for you, or you would not be on this journey with me. The world needs your ideas and contributions. You are on this Earth for a reason. You have a purpose to fulfill, and the power to do it. You must get on that flight, and do it now. When you use the power of urgency, you will unlock the door to a life of total success. You open that door and discover the secret of how you can have it all. The secret is simple—you start by doing it now.

DEVELOP AN ATTITUDE OF NOW

Do it now as if your life depended upon it; it just might.

URGENCY IS NOT the same as an emergency. If you deal with the urgent part of life, you will miss the emergency all together, saving valuable time. Most crises in life come from someone not taking action when they should have. When the *check engine* light in your car illuminates—fix it. Procrastinators put that light off until their engine fails on the freeway. Learning how to shift the *put off* to a *must do* by creating urgency will create a life of stability, balance and excitement.

*Most life problems are caused
by delaying what needs to be done today.*

WHEN TO EAT THE FROG FIRST

THIS CHAPTER MIGHT appear in conflict with my previously telling you to follow your passion first and the delay the things you don't want to do until later. This is going to take careful analysis on your part, and I know you can handle it. Here you go—

A check engine light will cause you problems if you delay fixing it. Checking email later will not leave you stranded on the freeway. A load of laundry waiting to be folded in the back room while you write your novel will not cause the bank to foreclose on your home, but not paying your mortgage will. There are things you must do today because they will impact tomorrow. The rest of the tasks that have no impact—put your goals first, and make them a must.

YOUR ONE CHANCE

WHEN I MOVED to the second officer position on a B747 and began training pilots, I noticed a pattern of performance, of delaying a task that resulted in problems. In earlier aircraft, pilots managed the fuel system (now the plane manages it) and a primary responsibility was to keep the fuel balanced. On the B747-200 fuel balancing was essential and timing critical. When a pilot looked at the fuel shortly *before* they *had to* manage it, the tendency was to wait until it was absolutely necessary. So they waited. Murphy's rule took over and something else came up that took the pilot's attention. By the time the pilot remembered and got back to their fuel system, the plane would be out of balance, sometimes critically so. As an instructor, I witnessed this often. Experience taught me that taking action early was far better than the *do it later* phenomena when you had a tendency to forget. Much of what we do in life is cue based. If the cue happens to be a thought before it's time, take action. That thought was your gift from the Universe. Develop the super power of doing it now.

"You must take action now that will move you towards your goals. Develop a sense of urgency in your life."
                                        -H. Jackson Brown, Jr.

CREATE LIFT

URGENCY CREATES LIFT enabling you to reach the level of success that you deserve. My strategy while working toward my PhD program was to attend part time so I could finish strong. There was no reason I needed to rush my education. During my first week of residency, I changed my mind.

My goal is to impact change in the aviation industry. I want be that person with experience inside operations to assist our government so we don't blindly react to situations by instituting regulations with ramifications that have not been clearly thought out, causing more problems. My goal needed to be done yesterday. Do you think I have time to doddle and do the five-year plan? It's much easier being part of the change than trying to undo what was done later. Knowing *why* you are focused on your goal will ignite a sense of urgency.

Your dreams are important, and you will make contributions that impact our world. You owe it to yourself, and society, to move forward with your dreams with grace, passion and enthusiasm. Use your power of urgency by turning on your afterburners.

TAKE ACTION NOW

- Find something that needs to be done, that you've been putting off and do it. Now.
- Read the book *The Power of Now* by Tony Robbins.

Joe was ecstatic about the great seats he had acquired to see his favorite team in game 7 of the World Series. He was surprised to see an empty seat next to him. He leaned over to the gentleman on the other side of the vacant seat and asked if someone was sitting there. The man responded that it was indeed unoccupied. Joe couldn't believe it. "Who in their right mind would miss this all important game?" he asked. The man responded, "Well actually the ticket belongs to me. My wife and I have shared these seats for as long as we've been married, and she passed away. This will be the first World Series we haven't attended together since our first year of marriage."

Joe responded, "I'm so sorry to hear that, but I have to ask, couldn't you find someone to take the seat? A friend, neighbor, or relative?"

The man just shook his head. "No, they're all at the funeral."

Chapter 11:

Commitment

*"Unless commitment is made, there are only
promises and hopes... but no plans."*
~Peter Drucker

*E*ND GAME is not just the title of Leland Shanle's third book—it's his life philosophy. His emphasis when training Air to Air Combat was, "Magnificent maneuvering is worthless without getting the shot. In a life application, that simply means getting the job done. No excuses, no whining—job done. In a dogfight, if you don't get the job done, you die. Period."

That philosophy was not always met with open arms in his politically correct world of the Navy. Leland said, "A Navy Commander was debriefing me on my shortcomings, years ago. With disdain the commander said, "Your problem is that you are results oriented." He went on to explain that it was all about the show and how you present yourself. In short—politics." Leland decided he would avoid organizations with that type of attitude. He gravitated toward the flight test world, where he built the reputation of quietly getting the job done. In a results-oriented field such as flight test, his commitment gave him power and strength.

> *"Individual commitment to a group effort—*
> *that is what makes a team work, a company work,*
> *a society work, a civilization work."*
> ~Vince Lombardi

Since the Navy, Leland has written six books, helped to set up airlines, has been an advisor on five movies and is the head of Broken Wing, a company that put together the discovery documentary *Plane Crash*. Most importantly he says, "I've had a lot of fun." He believes in getting the job done, and lived the power of commitment while standing true to his character. Imagine if he had morphed into a clone for the "image." Goal driven, Leland created a strategy by moving into flight test and built powerful habits of focus along the way. He used urgency to complete the tasks, lived his truth, and created opportunities that have designed a life of success. This is what the journey to success is all about!

> *Anything is possible if you have...*
> *The courage to Dream, The willingness to Learn,*
> *Dedication to Persevere, Commitment to Follow Through,*
> *And Never Give Up*

BECOME COMMITTED TO YOUR PURSUIT OF EXCELLENCE

WHAT IS THE DIFFERENCE between dedication and commitment? When a chicken and a pig are making ham and eggs for breakfast—the chicken is dedicated, the pig is committed.

Commitment and dedication may be used interchangeably, but there is a subtle difference. You might dedicate a song to a friend. But when you invest your time, energy, and creativity to writing that song, you have shifted from a dedication to a commitment. Commitment is giving more of yourself than you thought possible. It means not backing out when times are tough. It means once you are airborne, you have no option but to land. On this journey there is no backing out, turning, running, or quitting. When you make the decision to become committed to your dreams and your vision for your life, you don't stop.

> *"Desire is the key to motivation, but it's determination and commitment to an unrelenting pursuit of your goal —a commitment to excellence— that will enable you to attain the success you seek."*
> ~Mario Andretti

TURN YOUR DESIRES INTO COMMITMENTS

I ALWAYS WANTED to write a book, but not until I became fully committed to learning how to write was I able to do it. Saying I wanted to write was one thing, but only by pulling a credit card out of my wallet and paying lots of money for a writer's conference and buying an airline ticket (taking action) to Hawaii, did I turn my desire into a commitment. Stepping on the non-stop flight toward the conference furthered that commitment. But the true commitment came when I signed a contract to write fifty pages a week.

William Bernhart, my instructor at the writer's conference, is also an attorney. He gave me a contract that I filled out describing the level of commitment I was willing to dedicate to my work. We both signed it. He was a bit skeptical at my overzealous commitment, but I soon showed him that this was possible. Signing that contract elevated my level of commitment. That framed contract sat on my desk while I wrote and now hangs on my office wall. This contract gave me a daily goal. Bill wasn't sure if I could do it. But I knew if I did what I said, I would have a book within three months. A rough draft yes, but there would be a book! I could do anything for three months. William Bernhardt gave me the skills to write fiction, but he also gave me the tools to become fully committed in the form of a contract.

Another student, Heather McCorkle, became so committed that she quit her job to write full time. Such a leap wasn't easy for her, but she knew in her heart that writing was what she was meant to do, and she is fortunate enough to have the support and commitment of her husband to be able to do so. Through hard work, preparation, and courage, she followed her passion.

> *"Courage lies in our ability to develop a whole new mind set, skill set and heart set that optimizes the unbridled passion, purpose and potential of humans to do better, rather than simply living or woking faster than ever before."*
> -Irene Becker

Heather struggled like many writers, attending conferences, workshops, entering contests, constantly improving her skills, and yet she never quit when times grew challenging. Her first two books were with two different literary agents, and though they failed to sell, she did not give up. She became an independent author— indie. After extensive editing, she published five fantastic books and landed on the Amazon bestselling lists more than once. Three years after that first indie book, via hard work and commitment, her 10th manuscript placed second in a contest and she signed with two fantastic literary agencies. She has written 7 books since 2009, all because of commitment.

Commitment means moving beyond your security and comfort, sometimes waking up at 3 a.m., and throwing yourself into your dreams. It means changing your life from walking down a well-known path to changing directions and running into the unknown. It means investing time, money, and energy, or whatever it takes to make your flight a success. You are not wasting money if you are investing in yourself. You are worth every penny.

PERSEVERANCE + COMMITMENT = SUCCESS

REMEMBER ROB who started behind the power curve in his career? His success was due to commitment and perseverance. Following that first rejection from the Air Force, he earned his private, instrument, and commercial ratings while completing 36 hours of undergraduate studies. He went on to earn a master's degree in instruction and curriculum design, and earned a 3.7 GPA while working a full time job in an aircraft instrument repair facility. He flew at night to build flight time and logged almost 300 hours in complex aircraft. His application was denied by the Air Force pilot board during the first round; with the second round scheduled 90 days later. During that time period, he called every Air National Guard and Air Force Reserve Squadron in the country. Within 30 days he had eight interviews scheduled, but was hired on his first interview at the Air Guard Unit, 600 miles away from his home city.

Rob served twelve years in the West Virginia Air National Guard at the rank of Major. He was deployed to Bosnia, Iraq, and Afghanistan among other foreign nations and earned multiple medals including three Air Medals, four Aerial Achievement Medals, and two Meritorious Service Medals. He is happily married, with two sons, and is an airline pilot, writing his first novel, *Soldiers of God The Book of Lot.* Do you think Rob has contributed to the world?

KEEP FLYING!

PILOTS NEVER THROW their hands up in defeat while flying their plane. They fly all the way to the ground, doing everything possible to create a successful outcome, committed to getting their plane on the runway safely. Wilfred Parke, the first pilot to figure out how to get out of a spin did so at 50 feet. Imagine the result of his flight if he had become committed to being a passenger instead of flying the plane. What if he never shared that skill or if the pilots had not listened?

There exists a general aviation airplane designed with a parachute. If a pilot loses control in that aircraft, they can pull the parachute. The problem with flying through life with an easy button, like a chute to bail out when times get tough, is it will limit your level of success. There are no easy buttons in life. You must have the skills to fly your plane, and navigate your life toward success. Easy is not always the best. Skills will come with a commitment to excellence and perseverance during challenges along the way. When you become fully committed, you will learn what you need to know for the success you desire. Do not plan to bail out because you did not take the time to learn the necessary skills; be prepared.

Do you want your life to be a continued pursuit of bailouts, or do you want to finish your journey to success? Commit to what is important. I am not saying you must stick to a plan, because flexibility in life is essential. During your pursuit of excellence, you should have a backup plan. Pilots do. What I am saying is to commit to the life you want to live and learn through the struggles, instead of giving up because life got too hard. Learn how to shift with the wind and become flexible to opportunities. Do not jump out of a plane because you don't know how to fly. If you want to jump out of a plane, make that a choice, not because you forgot to get committed to taking flight lessons.

FIND WHAT DRIVES YOU AND COMMIT

"The quality of a person's life is in direct proportion to their commitment to excellence, regardless of their chosen field of endeavor."
-Vince Lombardi

NO MATTER HOW challenging the career of being a pilot became—bankruptcies, furloughs, mergers and acquisitions—my commitment held strong. Commitment is what it takes to achieve what you want in life. If you are committed to your journey, you will throw yourself into your passion. Your success will depend upon that level of commitment, and your willingness to never give up trying.

The only way you can fail is if you quit. So don't quit.

You can dance through life and have a great time. But when you truly commit to what you want, you will say your vows and hold strong. You will commit to the life you deserve and do what it takes to make it happen. You might be a 48-year-old woman giving up a six-figure income to become an airplane mechanic, or a seventeen year old that wants to become an artist. When you quit your job, or change majors from medical school to art school, family and friends might want to have you committed. But remember—this is *your* life. You are writing the story and you get to make the rules. Decide wisely.

FOLLOW THROUGH

ON MY HUSBAND's birthday we went to the driving range to hit golf balls. To put this event in context—he plays a little golf. I play none. I've played on a course maybe a handful of times and my visits to a driving range could fit in the other hand.

The first ball I whacked skidded across the range at an angle. The next three swings missed the ball entirely. The second ball fell off the tee. Frustrated, I decided to focus on a dimple on the ball. That's all I looked at. I never took my eyes off the dimple as I swung. I connected with the ball. Next I focused on a letter on the ball and smacked it again. I soon began to connect with the ball because I was keeping my eye on it. But the problem was the ball would not go straight. Every ball I hit angled to the left. I adjusted where I stood. But it didn't matter if I moved forward or back—the ball still went left. Then my husband said, "You need to follow through on your swing."

Ahhh—follow through.

Following through with your golf swing is a great metaphor for life. When we follow through on our plans, actions, and commitments, we achieve them. We hit straight and far. Following through with something is nothing more than giving it your all—all the way through.

One of my greatest strengths, and the reason I have been able to accomplish so much in my life, is my ability to follow through on commitments. When I say I'm going to do something—I do it. The more effort you give to something, the sweeter the success, and that feeling drives you toward the next project and fuels your ability to complete another. Success begets success.

BECOME ACCOUNTABLE TO YOUR GOALS

PILOTS ARE MISSION-DRIVEN people. Imagine if you arrived at the airport with the intent to take a flight to Hawaii, but your pilots decided the flight was too long, and the winds weren't right and they had something better to do. Not only would you miss your vacation, but those pilots would lose their jobs.

Pilots continue flying their plane no matter what the malfunction. They take off and land. They complete and follow through on the mission. Sometimes we may divert and other times delay due to weather and maintenance. But once we are in the air, we are committed to getting you and the plane safely on the ground. Airline pilots cannot function without commitment and follow through, and our passengers do not want us to. What if you viewed your commitments as a life and death obligation like flying a plane? How much more could you accomplish by committing fully?

Commitment is a choice,
and follow-through an action.
By harnessing the energy of both
there is nothing you cannot accomplish.

TAKE ACTION NOW

- Make a decision to become committed to your dream.
- Write down as many reasons as to why you must accomplish your goal.
- Take one action toward that goal.
- Watch the movie *In Pursuit of Happyness*.

A group of aircraft maintenance instructors were asked by the CEO to join him on a flight. After they all took their seats, they were informed that their students built the plane. All of the instructors jumped out of their seats and ran toward the exit, except one.

The CEO walked down the aisle and asked him why he remained. The man said, "If it was made by my students, I am confident it will not even start."

CHAPTER 12

CONFIDENCE

GO FORTH WITH CONFIDENCE TO GREATNESS

*"When you have confidence, you can have a lot of fun.
And when you have fun, you can do amazing things."*
                                                          -Joe Namath

"EVERGREEN 902, DO you have the runway in sight?"
Air traffic control (ATC) asked. I didn't, as it blended
in with the scattering of lights glowing in the night. The captain
responded, "We've got the runway in sight," as he pointed out the
window for my guidance, my eyes opened wide. The tower control
replied, "Cleared to land."

We were high and screaming in at 250 knots, gear and flaps up.
I was the pilot flying with less than fifty hours on the B727, and
what flashed through my mind was, *there is no way I can make this.*
As if he were reading my mind the captain said, "You can make it."
He had the experience, I didn't. I believed him and began configur-
ing my plane for landing. Thrust to idle. Flaps. Gear down. More

flaps. Arm the speed brakes. Checklist. Within minutes we were configured and landing safely.

The captain had confidence that I could make the runway because he was confident with his own ability. More than that, he gave me confidence. Not all pilots exhibited that behavior in those early days. They may have had confidence in themselves, but they were not about to make a female pilot's life any easier. Thankfully this captain was the exception. Twenty-eight years later I was flying with an A330 captain, and we discussed the performance of the first women pilots. He said, "I noticed later in my career that women the airlines hired were better pilots than the earlier gals."

I have no doubt he saw a difference, but it had nothing due to hiring better. The difference in performance he witnessed had everything to do with confidence. The early women were not welcome in the cockpit. They were harassed, propositioned with their jobs on the line, and strategically-placed pictures of naked women filled the cockpit. Many of the early women were not allowed to fly segments to gain the experience to become good. When they did fly, the guys decided to allow them to fly as a single pilot not providing standard crew support.

> *"If you have no confidence in self,*
> *you are twice defeated in the race of life."*
> -Marcus Garvey

How could anyone's performance be superior under those conditions, let alone be standard? Those early women were not provided the opportunity to gain that experience. Worse than that, confidence was shot down by the humiliation and destructive behaviors in the cockpit of the times, which further impacted performance. Thankfully times have changed and this behavior is no longer the rule. However, the lesson on confidence cannot be overlooked.

One of the many differences between male and female pilots that still lingers is the confidence level. Part of this difference is culture driven. Men tend to be more ego driven and won't show fear. Little boys would strut around the playground and tell the other boys how good they were. Little girls were taught modesty, with bragging looked upon unfavorably. These behaviors carried into their jobs and lives. Men also *do*, while women *want to understand* before they do.

When I told this captain my assessment between men and women he said, "We're all really just scared little boys and bury our fear deep within, allowing our ego to create our confidence. We create the confidence that we can, and then we go out there and do. Pretty soon, we are doing with success."

I asked, "If it's that easy, then why aren't we all burying our fears and faking it until we make it?"

He nodded and said, "Exactly. You don't know you can do it, unless you do it."

HOW CONFIDENT ARE YOU?

YOU MAY HAVE been emotionally beat up as a child and told you were nothing and wouldn't amount to anything. Maybe you came to that conclusion on your own because of a lack of ability while you were young. But those days and perceptions are behind you. Make a choice right now to believe in yourself. You can do anything, and the power of that belief will increase your confidence and accelerate your momentum.

There are two types of people who become successful—those that were told they could do anything and believed it, and those who were told they were worthless and *did not* believe it. Confidence is a choice—a choice that will determine your level of success. It doesn't matter how many people in your life have programmed you into thinking you are nothing. You are as good as you want to be. Reprogram your brain with the attitude of—*I can!* Because—you can.

TRUST YOURSELF

Before we can be truly great, we must trust in ourselves.

THE MORNING OF my B727 type rating—the test to determine if I would be a captain—began with nerves. Doubt crept into my mind. I was about to fly a three-engine jet and experience engine fires, hydraulic failures, an emergency descent, an emergency evacuation, and more. If that were not challenging enough, before my flight started I would sit with a federal aviation examiner and answer performance and system questions, then diagram the B727 electrical, hydraulic or air-conditioning system.

That morning I glanced at my manuals, there was nothing more they could provide short-term. There was a better way to prepare, to set myself up for success. The first step in preparing for this event began with logic. The instructor who authorized me to take this check had thousands of hours of experience and had trained hundreds of pilots. He would not have signed me off unless I was ready. His name and reputation were on the line too.

Many pilots with far more time and experience than I have failed. The question was *"Why had they failed if they knew what they were doing?"* Answer—nerves and misguided focus. I would not be one of those people. It was time for my power-walk. I drove to my local gym and walked the track talking to myself. I said, "I can do this! I've flown a perfect approach to minimums before, and I can do it again. I know all my procedures. I know how to fly. If I weren't ready, he would not have signed me off." I also talked through each procedure, visualizing each process.

You get the picture? I created a picture of success.

BELIEVE. ACHIEVE. SUCCEED.

THIS POWER-WALK INCREASED my level of confidence—I programmed my brain with an *I can* attitude, which replaced the fear. I had flown to standards the day prior during a practice ride. There was only one thing that could stop me—my mind.

You will be faced with similar performance events throughout your life. If prepared, there is only one thing that will destroy your success—allowing your mind to intervene with *what if I fail.* I showed up with confidence and passed my checkride. Was it perfect? Of course not. But when I made mistakes, I did not allow those errors to take down my confidence. Anyone can make errors, success comes from mitigating those errors so they do not compound into consequential failures. I kept my head and maintained confidence.

NO ROOM FOR PANIC

THERE IS NO room in your brain for confidence and panic to be present at the same time. You get one or the other. When you become stressed and allow your brain to react with panic—a fight or flight mode—you no longer think clearly because you can't. The rational and logical part of your brain won't function, thus you will *react* on an emotional level. Not necessarily the correct response.

Action and reaction are two different spectrums. Confident people take *action.* Those who lack confidence *react* to stimuli with emotion.

MAINTAIN CONFIDENCE AND TAKE ACTION

MAINTAIN CONFIDENCE so you will be the person who takes action. We are all scared at some point, but those who succeed use their skill and training to do the best they can because they *know* they can. They do not doubt, they *do*. They do not allow fear of failure to enter their thoughts. Pilots who keep their heads and remain confident in their abilities succeed.

You will be amazed at what you can accomplish if you first trust in yourself. Surround yourself with people who will enhance your confidence. The magnitude of what you can accomplish when you have the support of others is phenomenal. Build a strong team.

During my first checkride, I had finished all maneuvers and was beaming inside as I locked onto the ILS (instrument landing system) with an engine failure, sliding down the glideslope for my final event. Then I heard a voice behind me as my instructor said to the FAA examiner, "You should see her fly a raw data approach." Moments later the FAA examiner directed me to go around. Raw data means you are not following a flight director for guidance on an already complicated approach.

I had to make another approach, when I could have been done. This time they failed my flight director so I had to fly a raw data approach—with an engine failure! After we landed I said, "Thanks a lot!" and my instructor laughed. At the time I did not realize the confidence I received from that statement, "You should see her..." But that event was something I put in my flight bag and have carried with me throughout my career. When I begin to doubt, I hear Bo's voice. Why was I able to do that so early in my career? Because of skills I learned from Captain Corby.

What would happen if you put those words in your flight bag? You don't have to tell people how good you are. But what if you awoke each morning and told yourself there is nothing that you can't do! Set your day up for success by giving yourself the strength and confidence you deserve. When you hear it enough you believe it.

I had a captain throw his bags on the ramp, point his finger at me, and yell, "You don't belong in the cockpit!" His opinion—shrug it off. A first officer said, "You are taking a man's job who needs it to support his family." I have a family too—smile and nod. I also saw photos of naked women in the cockpit, but I figured this was their office before I came. That did not mean I could not set up my office. So one night on my freighter I replaced the female photos with naked men. The captain opened the compartment to check his escape rope and Miss March was replaced with a stud-muffin. He laughed and said, "Touché."

Having the confidence to deal with unusual and uncomfortable situations will arise in your life—take the challenge. This is not to say that the most confident person cannot be shaken. We are all shaken at some point. But shake it off and do better next time.

> *Performance and confidence are correlated*
> *—choose to be confident.*

Those early years when I flew with nervous pilots, I flew my worst. When I flew with confident pilots, I flew my best. Why would behavior and attitude of the other pilot impact my performance? We react to the level of confidence others have in us. Their lack of confidence degrades our performance because we assimilate it. The reason most people will behave as if they do not have confidence in you, is because they don't have confidence in themselves. Do not allow them to take yours too. Awareness is an amazing thing. Pay attention and you can shake off those feelings others place on you.

> *"Believe in yourself! Have faith in your abilities! Without a humble but reasonable confidence in your own powers, you cannot be successful or happy."*
> ~Norman Vincent Peale

BE YOUR BEST. DO YOUR BEST.

I SPEAK at aviation events and schools, but I never write a speech or have notes with me. Not because I have a great memory; the truth is I feel nervous talking in front of people. But I also know that when stressed our memory does not work like we want it to. We begin trying to remember what we are going to say versus just talking to the audience. To avoid forgetting what I plan on saying, I never write down the details ahead of time. More or less, I wing it.

Experience has proven that when I'm passionate and knowledgeable about what I'm talking about, momentum will carry the presentation. Each time becomes easier because I gain confidence from the previous experience. I still feel the nerves, but I come across as confident. I also never watch videos or listen to recordings of myself. Professionals say if you watch and listen to yourself, you can correct the flaws. But I speak from the heart. I have come to grips with an imperfect presentation of a perfectly passionate speech—confident that I am doing my best and with each experience becoming more confident in my ability.

After my second CNN event, I was ready for number three. This time I received more airtime. My confidence was higher than the first two. But when I was done, a girlfriend emailed and said, "Your make up was better last time. The lighting wasn't good, and I didn't like the tie." Talk about a confidence shaker. When you put yourself out there, critics will pop up from everywhere. Parents, friends, and coworkers will judge you. Heck, strangers will judge you. Some of that advice might be to help, but the reasons do not matter because the results are the same. Criticism will make you feel bad—but only if you allow it to. This too is a choice. Choose to be proud that you put yourself out there to be judged.

The higher you climb during your *Flight to Success*, the more critical people will become. Do not allow their comments to shake your confidence and throw you off balance. Your job in life is to learn from what they say, take what works, and thank them for their comments. Most of what people give you is a gift. The part that is not, drop kick it. Visualize kicking the words and them breaking apart. You'll be surprised at how little power they have—none.

TAKE CONTROL OF YOUR LIFE
AND YOUR CONFIDENCE WILL SOAR

MY PARENTS WERE divorced when I was nine. I was the middle of five daughters close in age and struggled for identity and control. Teachers told me what to do. My parents fought and told me what to do. My sisters told me where to go. I was not among the popular girls. I lived in a neighborhood where all my friends had new cars and fancy clothes, I didn't.

When I was 16, I borrowed a car and drove myself to the airport. I paid $15 for an introductory flight in a small plane. Once on the runway the instructor said, "You've got it." My response was, "No I don't. I can't fly!" as fear gripped me. "Yes, you can," he said. I took the controls and his voice guided me through the departure. As we lifted into the sky, I was one with the plane. I am telling you one thing, if you have never flown a plane, do it—if only for one flight. The confidence you gain will be worth every penny.

There is something about being in complete control while flying that changes your perception of life. The mixture of excitement with nerves, while defying gravity, combined with the hum of machine, as the world and all its problems pass by miles below, can be a most freeing experience. This flight hooked me and my dreams were cemented in the reality of possibility. More than that, earning a pilot's license while in high school gave me the confidence that I could do anything, despite many years of being told I couldn't.

Gratitude fills my heart as I had a mother who told me that I could do anything with hard work. I was also fortunate in my early years to have flown with a handful of confident and secure pilots who took pride in sharing their experience with me, to help me be the best I could be. Those are the experiences I allowed to define my life, not those people and events that attempted to tear me down.

CONFIDENCE IS A CHOICE

CONFIDENCE SHOULD BE your best friend on this journey. If you can make friends with it, holding it close to heart, you will be lifted beyond all possibilities. You will still experience fear when new opportunities and challenges arise. But with confidence holding your hand through life's ups and downs, you can do anything. It will lift you high and there will be nothing that you cannot do together.

TAKE ACTION NOW

- Change your language to the positive. Start believing in yourself.

- Find something that you have avoided because you lacked confidence. Then fake the confidence and go for it. The results will show you the power from faking it until you make it.
- Feeling adventuresome? Take a flight lesson.
- Watch the movie the *Blind Side*. Confidence can make a life.

Three people were sentenced to death. The executioner asked the first person, "Lethal Injection or Electric Chair?" The guilty party replied, "Lethal Injection." The shot was administered and the man died.

The second was asked the same question. He responded, "Electric Chair." The person sat in the chair and the switch was thrown, but nothing happened. The executioner said, "We have administered the punishment as per the law and you survived. You are free to go."

The executioner then turned to the third and asked, "Lethal Injection or Electric Chair?" The man replied, "Lethal Injection. The Electric Chair is obviously broken."

CHAPTER 13

EVALUATE

*"Take a step back, evaluate what is important,
and enjoy life."*

~Teri Garr

APPROACHING THE END of my two-year commitment with America West Airlines, they filed bankruptcy and furloughed everyone up through my class. They still needed instructors to conduct recurrent training, thus I stayed for what turned out to be another two years. I also instructed on the side for another company while enjoying the America West job, which was becoming easier with the same people, same procedures, etc. But easy is not my life and does not lead to growth. I had a revelation, or was getting restless, as a voice spoke to me and said, "It's time to move on." It was time to evaluate what I was doing.

SHAKE UP YOUR LIFE

MY PLAN WAS to become an airline pilot and fly. I loved teaching, but there was more to a pilot's life than a simulator. I learned what I could in those four years. I evaluated the situation and knew that my career would not be at America West Airlines. I wanted to fly around the world in a wide-body aircraft. It was time to move on.

If you hang out doing something that's just okay, waiting for the perfect job to come, you may wait for a very long time. Sometimes you need to shake up your life, add to your experience, and get back in the world so you will be available for the calling of your life. While I was entertaining the thoughts of stagnation, Guyana Airways called and offered a training job of another kind—to develop and implement an in-house training program.

While training the initial cadre of Guyana pilots, I learned from America West's mistakes because I evaluated what worked and what didn't. I took that knowledge to Guyana and created a program that enabled success for all.

The ability to evaluate yourself, your dreams, processes, and how you are conducting business will be a great asset throughout life. Growth and success is a continually evolving process. Nothing stays the same in life and neither will you. The monitoring process of evaluation will keep you on track, point you in another direction, or may encourage you to create a new plan altogether.

Evaluation is a key to situational awareness and airline safety. Pilots are always evaluating the environment. We make decisions based on what we see during this evaluation. Life success will be yours through careful evaluation of your circumstances, and taking appropriate action.

> *"A truthful evaluation of yourself gives feedback*
> *for growth and success."*
> ~Brenda Johnson Padgitt

As you gain momentum on your *Flight to Success* and move closer to your destination, be sure you are flying in the correct direction.

Have you made good decisions along the way? Did you program the correct flight plan? Are you sure this is the flight you want to be on? Will your flight be on time? Did you add enough fuel?

Pilots constantly keep an eye on fuel, speed, and weather. We are evaluating for one reason—to see if we are achieving our goals as planned. A successful flight includes paying attention to what's working and to fix what's not. If the headwind is too strong at our flight level, increasing fuel burn, we will find a more efficient cruising altitude.

AUTOMATION. EVALUATION. COMPLACENCY.

JUST LIKE AIRPLANES of today, your world is becoming increasingly automated. Many pilots depend upon this technology to take care of them and complacency sets in. Complacency is automation's evil twin. When everything is working, it's easy to allow attention to slide. When your life is working, complacency may make you miss important cues along the way.

On your *Flight to Success*, due diligence is required to make certain you are on the flight path and achieving the results you desire. Compliments of technology, your workload may reduce during your journey. Automated airplanes not only reduce workload, but they create a safer and more efficient operation. The problem begins with automation being so incredibly reliant that pilots follow it blindly without evaluating the process. They trust that their automated plane is doing what it was supposed to do, and will keep them safe. It does, until it doesn't. Evaluation is the only way to make sure you are heading in the correct direction in the most efficient manner.

On your journey to success you might get in the flow and begin running on autopilot. If you live life blindly, you could arrive at the end of the day wondering what happened and where the heck you landed. Your success on this journey will be indicative of your ability to step back and take a look at the big picture of your progress. Evaluate where you are, what you want, and if you are on the right path. By evaluating your environment you will avoid the thunderstorms of life.

HUMAN ERROR

HUMANS MAKE ERRORS. Errors are okay if we don't allow them to compound. Unfortunately an undetected error in an airliner can compound into a catastrophic accident. We want to believe that the captain of our plane is incapable of failure. The fact is, fatigue, flying the backside of the clock, multiple time zones, and night flying causes sheer exhaustion. Being awake for 17 hours is equivalent to an alcohol level of .05.

On your journey to success you will be living some crazy fatigue-induced schedules. Pilots and people alike are prone to errors. Therefore, we must continually evaluate our performance and that of our plane, and so must you. If a pilot follows his automated aircraft blindly through the hills, he may hit a mountain—it's happened. You must monitor and evaluate your life as if your success depends upon the outcome—because it does. Your life will depend upon monitoring your actions and results along the way. Are you where you want to be at a given time? Is your plan working or do you need to change something?

"True genius resides in the capacity for evaluation of uncertain, hazardous, and conflicting information."
                                                    ~Winston Churchill

EVALUATE YOUR DECISIONS ALONG THE WAY

WITHIN THE YEAR of writing this book, two sets of pilots landed at the wrong airport. The aviation world was baffled—how could they do that? Human factors had a strong hand in the results. What if those pilots had evaluated cues before they landed? Careful evaluation would have presented many opportunities that could have pointed them in the correct direction. In these cases no deaths occurred other than the egos and careers of very competent pilots. However, there was a freighter this same year that hit a hill while on final approach, killing both pilots. In an airline accident, it's never due to one thing. Competent humans missed a key aspect of success—evaluation.

TIME TO EVALUATE

AS YOUR LEVEL of success increases, so does life's complexity. Your life will be filled with all sorts of stress, especially if you're working toward a goal. You will also find it more difficult to find time to evaluate whether or not you are on the correct course. Taking time to evaluate will be paid back tenfold in reward. With evaluation you must also practice the skill of flexibility to deal with what you discover. When you mess up, solve the problem and move forward.

"A large portion of success is derived from flexibility. It is all very well to have principles, rules of behavior concerning right and wrong. But it is quite as essential to know when to forget as when to use them."
~Alice Foote MacDougall

BEND WITH THE FLOW OF LIFE

LIFE IS ABOUT motion. When we stop bending, soaring, and lifting our faces to possibility—we break. Make a commitment to become flexible. Your journey to success began with a goal—a vision that pointed you one direction in pursuit of accomplishing your dream. But this journey called life will take many paths, twists, and turns. The initial step down that path will get you started. Where you go from that initial dream will be predicated by the decisions you make along the way. Sometime your direction will be of necessity because life threw something in your path. Other times you are exposed to a passion greater than the first. One guarantee—life will unfold as you live it. Doors will open if you are willing to shift, change, and work to go through them.

Evaluate and then…

BE OPEN AND WILLING TO CHANGE

WHEN I WROTE my first novel I outlined the story. But not until the characters took on life and found their way through the twists and turns of the plot, did I find the essence of the plot—it changed along the way. The ending changed too. The only reason *Flight For Control* became a breakout novel was because I was flexible and willing to listen, learn, and change my thinking.

Flexibility in life goes beyond writing. A quality life is about working with others—family, friends, and coworkers. There are times you might have to ask if being right is more important than the relationship that it may destroy. Evaluate that decision carefully.

There are other times you have to stand firm on your decision, but each situation will be unique to your life. Once you start paying attention to the art of being flexible, you will know when those times arise and when to stand your ground or change your opinion. There may be times when you realize that a situation is contradictory to your health and happiness and you don't want to be involved. Careful evaluation might just tell you to remove yourself from that situation, get another job, or find a new friend.

Pilots are mission-driven people. And yet there are times when we must divert to another airport. This decision-making ability is one of the qualitative judgments instructors look for during a checking event—how does the pilot deal with unexpected outcomes? They see, evaluate, and become flexible to changing their original plan.

LISTEN AND BE WILLING TO ADAPT

CREW RESOURCE MANAGEMENT (CRM) came about to teach crewmembers how to work together after the industry learned accidents occurred when we all thought the captain could do no wrong. As much as we learned communication skills with CRM, the pilot in the left seat also learned the power of working with and listening to others, and evaluating the environment.

I recently read a great story in the book *The Pilot Factor*, by Jean Marcellin, about an incident when an engine caught fire in their aircraft, while the plane sat on the ramp. Flames shot past the cockpit and in front of the emergency exit. The captain's first reaction was to evacuate. The first officer suggested they continue to run the engine in attempt to put out the fire. The captain acknowledged that his first officer's idea was brilliant, and they extinguished the flames.

Prior to the onset of CRM, this first officer might have been reluctant to say anything to his captain. And if he had, the captain may have stuck to his decision because it was his decision and nobody was going to tell him what to do—a time when captains were *always* right, even when they were wrong. This is a great story for many reasons, but mostly this example demonstrates the power of evaluating conditions and being flexible. Evaluation and listening can keep your passengers from being cooked while you're trying to save them. You don't always *have* to be right, when you are flexible. Surround yourself with intelligent and creative people, evaluate your life, be willing to listen to what others have to say, become flexible with your decisions, and you will increase your opportunity of reaching success ten-fold.

> *"The mind that opens to a new idea*
> *never returns to its original size."*
> ‑Albert Einstein

COMMIT TO EVALUATION AND FLEXIBILITY

AS YOU CONTINUE your journey, make a commitment to be flexible for what life throws your way. You are writing your story. But not until each chapter plays out will you have an idea what the next chapter will bring. Pay attention and be willing to stand for what you believe in, but also flow and move with what comes your way. Listen and learn. Keep your mind open and train yourself to evaluate.

The art of evaluation and being flexible will expose you to new ideas. You will listen to others and work for a common good. When you are willing to move with the flow of life, you open the doors of opportunity. Life is filled with opportunity. The question is if you are ready to free your thinking and become flexible by shifting your processes. If you are, there is no stopping you.

"Stay committed to your decisions,
but stay flexible in your approach."
~Tony Robbins

TAKE ACTION NOW

- Take a close look at the strategy you built, then add time intervals to regularly check on your progress.
- At the completion of each interval, look at the current environment and determine if your plan is still valid. For example, if the rules changed and you don't need a flight engineer rating, then remove that from your plan of action.
- Pay attention to your flexibility. If there is another way, a better way, be open to change. Don't get so committed to the plan that you forget the goal. Evaluate, and if there is a better route, take it.
- Watch the movie *The Shawshank Redemption*. Imagine finding your life turned upside down with false accusation of murder, and ending up in prison. Survival depends upon evaluating your circumstances and adjusting for survival.

A new pilot, Dan, was working hard to build his proficiency in all aspects of flight. He felt he mastered all but one. His landings were inconsistent, with some being smooth as glass, and others like he was landing on an aircraft carrier. He found his instructor preparing for the next student, and asked him for advice. The instructor said, "It's about establishing the right power settings, the right pitch angle, the correct speed, and staying focused on the landing spot." He hesitated for a moment then added, "Don't lose focus on that landing spot. That's where most pilots make the mistake."

Dan thanked the instructor and climbed back into his plane to practice. The instructor decided to watch and provide feedback via the radio. As Dan set up for the first landing, the instructor noted the landing gear was not down. "Remember to lower your gear," the instructor said over the radio. As the plane descended, the gear remained up. "Cessna 23547, lower your gear!" The instructor yelled, followed by "Dan! Lower your landing gear!" But Dan never lowered the gear and the plane landed gear up destroying the bottom of the airplane, the propeller, and the engine.

Thankfully, Dan wasn't hurt, but as he stepped out of the plane, the instructor yelled, "Didn't you hear me telling you to lower the gear?" Dan responded, "I did what you said, and stayed focused on my landing spot. But I couldn't hear anything over the radio because there was a loud horn going off in the cockpit."

CHAPTER 14

SINGLE-MINDED FOCUS

WHAT YOU FOCUS ON BECOMES YOUR REALITY

"Successful people maintain a positive focus in life no matter what is going on around them. They stay focused on their past successes rather than their past failures, and on the next action steps they need to take to get them closer to the fulfillment of their goals rather than all the other distractions that life presents to them."

-Jack Canfield

MY NERVES RUMBLED with the idle of the engines as I released the brakes and pushed the thrust levers toward full power. My heart rate sped in direct proportion to the acceleration of the B737 as we flew down the runway. Then all hell broke loose. Bells rang, a fire handle illuminated bright red, and the first officer yelled, "Engine failure!" as the power rolled back to idle, and the plane yawed to the left. Maintaining control of my plane, hugging the centerline, my eyes flashed to the airspeed indicator confirming we could stop on the remaining runway. I simultaneously pressed the brake pedals and yanked the thrust levers to idle. After pulling the speedbrake lever aft, my hand flew to the thrust reversers and I yanked them into full reverse.

When the fire occurred, we were ten knots below decision speed for takeoff—meaning an abort was preferable to taking the plane into the air. During the abort, my eyes had darted to the brake pressure indicator—zero. *What?!?* Our normal brakes were gone. We had pressure during the preflight. *Didn't we?* I had looked at it during the checklist response. *Didn't I?* I was sure of it.

The engine failure occurred in a simulator during my type-rating checkride. Part of this check included an interior preflight—a visual scan of the instruments, overhead panel, and systems that included moving switches into position and assuring the plane was ready for flight. Prior to any checking event, FAA examiners hide *Easter eggs*. An Easter egg in a simulator is nothing more than low oil pressure, depleted hydraulics systems, or an inoperative flight instrument; something to show that the pilot could identify the abnormal situation, and take care of it appropriately.

On this particular day I found a few miscellaneous items. Once I dealt with them I called for the preflight checklist. The first officer read and I responded to each item, confirming the plane was ready to go. One of those items was "break pressure." Which I acknowledged with, "Checked." We started engines, performed the remaining checklist items, taxied onto the runway and received our takeoff clearance.

Examiners never give an engine failure as the first event. There was only one reason I had an engine failure prior to my first departure—I had screwed up and missed that brake-pressure gauge sitting at zero.

FOCUS ON THE TASK AT HAND

SYD BLUE WAS determined to become a pilot. She began taking lessons in an old beat-up plane with an even older flight instructor. She was terrified he would conk out, or the old plane would fall apart while learning to fly. Syd said, *"I had to drum up courage before each flight."* Then one day flying solo, as a student pilot, she got caught in un-forecasted winds—Santa Anas.

These winds could take down the best pilots. The turbulence was strong and she was violently tossed up and down. Exceeding the critical angle of attack, the plane stalled every few seconds, which she responded to by gently correcting the angle. How did she survive? Focus. She focused on flying her plane, not on the fear she felt. Her thoughts were not on *what if*. Not on pending death. Her focus was only on flying the plane, and thus the reason for her success.

Syd is no novice to what single-minded focus can do for success in all areas of her life. She used the power of focus to write the books *FlyGirl* and *Circle*, buy an airplane, and start her own aviation business. She is living her dreams because of her ability to focus on what she wants, not what she fears.

Where you place your focus will determine your outcome.

During that abort, my focus centered on stopping the airplane, and a fire that needed to be extinguished. Zero brake pressure could have impacted the success of stopping my aircraft, but it did not have to. I knew enough about the B737 that I could stop the plane with only the hydraulic accumulator system available. I managed a perfect abort procedure under the conditions. Once the engine was secured and checklists complete, I took a big breath waiting for the decision to come crashing down—continue with the checkride or stop right then and accept a pink slip for my failure.

"What happened?" The FAA examiner asked.

"We had an engine fire."

"Anything else?"

"As I aborted, I noticed we didn't have any brake pressure. But we did have the accumulator, so I applied the brakes with smooth but firm pressure."

"How many applications do you have with the brakes on the accumulator?"

"About six, but it's best not to pump them."

The FAA inspector repositioned our aircraft to the departure end of the runway and our checkride continued, ending in success. I became a B737 captain that day. The only reason I succeeded after I had made such a huge error was my ability to focus on what was necessary at the time, not on the failure. The error had been made and I could not undo that. However, I knew that I could stop my aircraft, put out the fire, and deal with my error appropriately because I was prepared. During the continuation of the checking event I focused on the ensuing events, not on the mistake I had made.

The examiner said he was surprised the ride turned out like it did. He thought that the lack of hydraulic brake pressure—which had been there from the moment I entered the simulator—would have been the beginning of the end. He had seen more times than not, that when a pilot made one error they would focus on that error instead of what they were doing, which would ultimately end in a failed checkride. Had my focus been on the error(s) I made, missing the indication—not once but twice—I would have been thinking about what was going on behind me, not on flying the plane.

"Don't dwell on what went wrong. Instead, focus on what to do next. Spend your energies on moving forward toward finding the answer."
~Denis Waitley

Imagine you are walking across a river and slip on a stone, but you make it safely to the next rock. If you focused on that first misstep and what was behind you, not on the next step in front of you, you wouldn't make it very far without getting wet. This is the same principle in reaching success in anything you do—focus on what you are doing at the moment, and not on what you have done. There is a time and place for reflection—but not while you are in the process of a task.

KEEP YOUR VISION IN FOCUS

ONE OF THE most important tasks on your journey to success is to keep your vision—your driving force—in focus. You must also be able to zoom in on the tasks that will lead you to that goal.

Imagine a mountain off in the distance as your goal. You point your camera on the sight, take a picture, and post it on the wall—your vision. The dream is to climb that mountain. How you will get there is your strategy. The first obstacle is a river to cross. You will either fear the river and never try, or you can push your limits and take the challenge to cross it. Focus management becomes a dance. The more you practice placing your focus where it belongs, the better you will get. This dance will become natural as you fly through life.

There are two areas, however, that you should never place your focus—worry and fear. Focusing on these thoughts wastes valuable brain cells needed for performance, and *will* destroy your chance for success. You cannot be effective with a task if your mind is elsewhere. Rocks that fly up and take out your prop will be self-induced. Do not worry about failure while you are performing. Have confidence that if the failure occurs you will deal with it at that time. Besides, if your head is in the right place, you won't fail.

SEE IT AND BELIEVE

FOCUS ON THE mountain you want to climb and take the picture. Take a photo of the airplane you want to fly and the uniform you want to wear. Take a picture of the joy you want in your life. Whatever your dream might be, create a picture. If you don't know what you want, then write the word belief, dream, success, family, or future on a piece of paper. Or better yet, make up something. As you have learned through this journey to success—life changes, and so will you. The vision you embark on today might not be your final destination. Be prepared to divert. But you must have a destination that you are moving toward—your vision. Your focus.

A secret of achievement is moving forward

If you don't know what you want in life, you could pick anything for your vision. The key is to be headed toward a destination. One guarantee in life—if you don't know where you are going you will never get there. Pick a dream, and as you work toward that dream your ultimate passion will come to light along the way. For now, hang your vision on the wall. Make it the first thing you see in the morning and the last thing you see at night. Whatever your vision—your *Flight to Success* will get you there.

YOU GET WHAT YOU FOCUS ON

FOCUS ON WHAT you desire not what you fear. What if I had failed my checkride? Would thinking about that during my flight have enabled me to perform any better? Of course not. It would only have been a distraction that turned into a self-fulfilled prophecy. I have seen "*checkrideitis*" many times throughout my career—those people who do fabulously until they are under scrutiny of an examiner. Why do they mess up when someone is watching? They are focusing on the person standing behind them and not on flying the plane.

When you have made that commitment to take your life test, concentrate on what is happening, not what might happen.

I have been asked numerous times, "Don't you worry about all those passengers when you fly?" I always reply, "Of course not." A pilot's focus is always on flying the plane, not in passenger cabin. There is a time and place when you can shift your focus. That time is never during a critical task. Do not live your life worrying about what is going on behind you. One of the most useless things a pilot could think about is the runway left behind.

The past is over while the present is a gift to be opened.

FOCUS ON THE PRESENT

EQUALLY AS DYSFUNCTIONAL as focusing on what if you fail, is focusing on the past. Focusing on the past prevents you from enjoying the present and living in the now. Thinking about a life you left behind wastes time and sucks energy. Focusing on the negative kills the joy of living, and creates distraction. Live today and tomorrow with joy and excitement. Focus on the present as this is your gift to the future.

"We can always choose to perceive things differently. You can focus on what's wrong in your life, or you can focus on what's right."
-Marianne Williamson

LEARN FROM YOUR PAST—DON'T LIVE THERE

FIND ONE SUCCESSFUL person who has had a perfect life and I will show you twenty who did not. Blaming your history, your hardships, and all that came before, diminishes your potential of success. Reliving a challenged past will emotionally take you there and keep you locked in a life you don't want. It's time to break free and escape those thoughts. Decide right now that you no longer will live in that place.

Most people could tell you about a troubling life event. They were born into a dysfunctional family, lost a family member or friend, experienced a less than desirable relationship, lost a business or invested poorly. I am positive you can add to that list with something you wish you could change. Negative past events are nothing but baggage. This baggage is not needed for your trip to success. As a matter of fact, the added weight will impact your level of success. Everything that has happened in the past—good and bad—has brought you to where you are today—physically, emotionally, and mentally. Release it. Let it go. Get on your with your life.

Today is perfect and the beginning of tomorrow.

FIND YOUR BEST ALTITUDE

AN AIRLINER'S INITIAL cruise altitude is lower than the final altitude because planes are heavier on departure. As the aircraft's weight is reduced due to fuel burn, the plane can climb to a higher altitude where performance is significantly improved. Imagine if these flights carried no baggage. Leaving all that weight behind, they could climb immediately to 41,000 feet and attain the best performance, saving fuel, time, energy, and arrive at the destination faster. *What if you left your baggage behind?*

Mental baggage will hold you down on your *Flight to Success*. If I had wasted time wishing what *could have* been, I would not be where I am today. I would not have the friends, experiences I learned from, or eight airline's worth of data to write about. My life, energy, and attitude come from living fully in the moment and focusing on today and the future—not living somewhere behind me. Everything we do changes what's to come. Learn from the past and get on with your life. Everything that has happened has made you the person that you are today and has brought you to this moment. Focus on the picture on your wall. Focus on what you are doing. Focus on something powerful and positive.

FOCUS ON TODAY AND YOUR FUTURE.

"The direction of your focus is the direction your life will move. Let yourself move toward what is good, valuable, strong and true."
-Ralph Marston

FOCUS ON FLYING YOUR PLANE

IN 1972 a tragic airline accident occurred because an Eastern Airline's crew focused on a burnt out light bulb and did not notice that their autopilot had disconnected. The plane slowly descended into the Everglades killing 101 people. These highly-trained pilots focused on the wrong thing and no one was flying the plane.

Flying the plane is the first priority when pilots deal with any emergency. Your level of success will depend on your ability to focus on priorities. You must zoom in on that stone you're about to step on to cross the river in pursuit of your dream. When *preparing* for an interview, focus only on what you will say—not what will happen if they turn you down. Focus on the flight you are on, not the runway left behind.

Focus takes practice, but when you pay attention, it becomes easier with each flight.

TAKE ACTION NOW

- Find a vision and put it on your wall, or better yet close your eyes and see it. If you can visualize with clarity, your brain cannot distinguish the difference.

- Bring your picture of success into focus each morning. During the day, focus only on what you are doing. Your vision will not go anywhere—it will be waiting for you to take another look at the end of the day.

- Pay attention to your thoughts. When your mind goes someplace you do not want it to travel, say, "I am not going there." Eventually your mind will listen and those events will occur less often. This could occur while sitting in an airplane ready for departure and thinking about the fight you had with a friend; or trying to study while your mind drifts to how you will pay for school. Don't go there. Think about what you are doing at the moment and be present.

- Practice. Like anything else, you will get good at controlling your focus the more you practice.

- Watch the movie *Invictus*.

Focus is your guiding light.
Illuminate the outcome of your desires,
as where you shine the beam,
will create your reality.
The power is yours, use it wisely.

A college student was sitting in Starbucks studying, and opened a letter he'd received that morning from his mom. As he opened it, a twenty-dollar bill fell out. Looking out the window. He noticed a beggar sitting on the ground, leaning against a light post. Thinking that the poor man could probably use the twenty dollars more than he, he crossed out his name on the envelope and wrote across the top in large letters, PERSEVERE!

He put the envelope under his arm and dropped it as he walked past the man. The man picked it up and read the message and smiled. The next day, as the young man's head was in his books, the beggar came into the coffee shop, tapped him on the shoulder, and handed him a wad of bills.

Surprised, the student asked him what that was for. The man replied, "This is your half of the winnings. Persevere came in 1st in the fourth race yesterday and paid thirty to one."

CHAPTER 15

STRENGTH

**PERSEVERE THROUGH FAILURES, CHALLENGES, AND
SETBACKS. THROUGH THIS STRENGTH
YOU CAN ACCOMPLISH ANYTHING**

*"Susanne died on July 17th, 1996.
She was my fiancée, she was thirty-one,
and it goes without saying, she was the love of my life."*
~Mark L. Berry

SUSANNE WAS ONE of 230 passengers and crew on board
TWA Flight 800 when it was blown up offshore Long Island,
and the end of their lives was also the end of many others. It could
have been the end of Mark's too, but it wasn't.

*"For ten years I wandered the Earth: playing touch-and-go
with feeling people's hearts—and I even circled the
planet once—but endless days came and went,
and they didn't mean anything…"*
~Mark L. Berry

Family and friends saw the empty shell Mark's life had become. He was a pilot for TWA at the time, and his airline grounded him. When he was released back to the flight line, he went through the daily motions of life without living. He was a ghost that wandered the world, empty, but existing. It wasn't until Mark began making music and writing did life slowly come back. But when Professor Schwartz, from the University of Missouri, St. Louis, recommended he tackle TWA 800 directly, the skies opened. Mark locked himself away, and was finally able to dig deep into that night, recounting it on paper for the first time, thirteen years after it happened.

> *"A counselor I saw at TWA, to address my grief, once told me that feelings we bury, we bury alive. Mine came crawling back out."*
> ~Mark L. Berry

I had been flying a B747 with Tower Air at the time. That night my plane was to trail TWA 800 to Paris. I watched the explosion, unsure at the time what had transpired until well into the night.

It wasn't until years later that Mark and I crossed paths. His story, *13,760 Feet—My Personal Hole in the Sky,* is an amazing reflection of resilience and strength. Today Mark is flying as a captain, living a life Susanne would be proud of. His has been a long journey, and he not only survived, but thrived to great success. I asked him what message of strength and resilience he could share, if any.

Mark said, "Whatever you are facing, don't let yourself become discouraged. Sometimes the road to a better place is long, but unless you are content to remain unhappy where you are—either literally or emotionally—the effort you eventually put into your own personal growth is worth it."

As it turned out, the writing and music that led Mark out of his hole and back into the world has turned out to be a talent like none other. Mark's success comes from resilience and strength, proving that good things are just around the corner no matter what.

Hopefully on your journey you will not face this kind of loss, but you might. Your level of success will depend on how you deal with the setbacks along the way, as well as those insurmountable challenges, and never giving up.

You may have been challenged the moment you were born. Jessica Cox entered the world without arms, yet she earned a pilots license. She told me that if she could live her life over, she would not want arms. This challenge, that initially brought tears and a fear of what her future would hold, became one of her greatest gifts. Jessica is proof that we do not need arms or wings to fly if we have inner strength and perseverance.

One of my greatest challenges with resilience was when my middle daughter was paralyzed at 21-years-old, and I hoped she had the strength to power through this life challenge. At one point my mother called me in tears and said, "Kayla's going to be okay, she will walk again." It was those words that gave me insight as to why I was holding it together—my daughter did not *need* to walk to be okay. She was going to be okay as long as there was life because of her strength. Her life would have been different, but she would have been okay. There is power in that belief, as there is power in being resilient.

"Nothing in this world can take the place of persistence. Talent will not: nothing is more common than unsuccessful men with talent. Genius will not: unrewarded genius is almost a proverb. Education will not: the world is full of educated derelicts. Persistence and determination alone are omnipotent."
-Calvin Coolidge

NEVER GIVE UP

DURING YOUR JOURNEY, focus will give you direction. But perseverance, resilience, and strength will fuel your *Flight to Success*. Strength has nothing to do with your muscle mass, but everything to do with your resolve, devotion, and determination—your resilience. Things will go wrong, but if you persevere and have the ability to deflect your emotions when things don't go your way—and don't give up—you will succeed. Success is not determined by the failures you experience, but how you deal with those failures.

I had flown with the most uplifting captain I had met in a long time, Victor Wagoner. His attitude was one of positivity, and nothing that occurred in his life, no matter how bad, did he bemoan. He accepted responsibility for his actions, felt compassion for others, and he believed it was *all good*. He was a swimmer and an overall athlete; coached junior high football on his days off; has a great marriage with children and grandchildren; and loved his job as an airline captain. So when I heard he was in a motorcycle accident and lost his lower leg, and almost his life, I wondered if he would maintain the positive attitude.

It's easy to be happy and positive when life goes your way. But to have the world ripped out from under you, and still keep smiling, now that takes strength. When I finally talked to Victor, he said, "It is what it is. I'll be back flying soon." Yes, the same positive attitude prevailed.

While battling infection and setbacks, he focused all his attention on health in order to return to flying. Not only learning to walk by mastering his new leg, but he had to learn to manage the rudders to fly. One of his greatest challenges would be getting his medical back.

Within 11 months he reached his health and professional goals, demonstrated flight performance, and received a new medical certificate. He was back flying an A330 prior to the first anniversary of his accident. *Who does that?* Someone with incredible strength and resilience, focused determination, a clear vision, and a ton of commitment where failure is not an option.

Your attitude will determine your altitude. Had Captain Wagoner focused on *what if* he couldn't make it back, and the pain and effort it would take, he would still be grounded. You have this kind of strength too, all you have to do is find the right attitude and go with it.

"Failure should be our teacher, not our undertaker. Failure is delay, not defeat. It is a temporary detour, not a dead end. Failure is something we can avoid only by saying nothing, doing nothing, and being nothing."
–Denis Waitley

CHALLENGE YOURSELF

THOSE WHO DO not fear failure design a life that assures success. Success is doing the best you can *despite* your failures. Surviving a horrific episode in your life, coming out on the other side, and sharing it with the world to help others in your situation. Avoiding failure will create a safe and boring life—not a successful life. When you give up opportunities because you don't want to fail, you also give up the opportunity to learn from the failure itself. Failure leads to opportunities of growth and unlimited potential.

"Failures are finger posts on the road to achievement."
–C. S. Lewis

FAILURE BUILDS STRENGTH

ONE OF MY greatest secrets to success is that I do not fear failure. Of course I don't want to fail, but I don't allow the fear of failure to stop me. I do the best I can to prepare and then ask, "What's the worse thing that could happen if I fail?" Usually it's nothing more than the humility of being human. The truth is—failure is one of the best educators we can have in our lives. Failure builds unlimited strength.

BREAK FREE FROM THE NEED TO BE PERFECT

As A B747 second officer check airman, my annual training occurred in December. All instructors were the first to experience the ensuing year's training program. We checked each other. Everyone had the "gouge" as to what the events entailed so we could all prepare and not look stupid in front of each other. I never looked at the scenario beforehand. My students did not get to see it, so why should I?

I did not fear failing this event. The power of learning outweighed a need to show my fellow instructors some illusion of perfection. I know I'm not perfect and I certainly don't need to be such. My goal in life is to see what I'm capable of after preparation during the big test called life. I *wanted* to know what I didn't know before I climbed into that B747. I wanted to be exposed to what my students were exposed to without privileged information. I needed to see what kind of mistakes I would make, so I could anticipate theirs. I wanted to share my experience when they made similar errors. How could pre-knowledge be more powerful than showing up as if I were in the student's shoes?

The outcome of all instructors being perfect was a façade. The only reason they were perfect was because they knew what was coming. Life is not that clear. We do not get an outline of what will happen next in life. Playing it safe is a placebo. You don't really get to avoid the hardships. Prepare. Be confident. Do your best. Those who prepare and take action, despite the fact they might fail, are the people who will find the greatest success in life. Have the strength to learn and bounce back when things don't go your way. This is about being resilient. This is the essence of strength.

> *"Only those who dare to fail greatly*
> *can ever achieve greatly."*
> -Robert F. Kennedy

FAILURE LEADS TO SUCCESS

I SPENT TWENTY-TWO years instructing pilots, and every day I looked forward to the possible errors my students would make in the simulator. Not because they would be judged, but because they would learn and become better pilots. More times than not, I would learn too. Nobody is perfect and when perfection showed up in training, I always wondered on which flight they would face the unexpected and their first failure—could they handle it? Would they be prepared?

To watch a student make an error and see how they handled the problem, and what that error did to the remainder of the flight, also told me what kind of pilot they were and gave an excellent indication of what they were capable of, indicating their mental strength. Failure is a great benchmark for success. Success means when you fall on your face, you have the strength to get back up. Success is about learning and growing from your failures, not avoiding them.

*"When we give ourselves permission to fail,
we, at the same time, give ourselves permission to excel."*
~Eloise Ristad

HOW YOU HANDLE FAILURE
WILL DICTATE YOUR LEVEL OF SUCCESS

THREAT AND ERROR management is one of my favorite aviation safety models. Pilots know that mistakes will occur—just as in life. We prepare and do our best, but we also know the unexpected might happen. We do not cancel flights because it's raining at our destination and we're afraid we might have to go to our alternate. We prepare by adding extra fuel. We press forward and take a look when we arrive and handle the situation at the time. Pilots do not prepare for failure—they plan for contingencies.

The threat and error safety model trains us to open our eyes to all the possibilities that could lead to failure, which creates awareness. The key is to identify potential situations that could lead to errors and manage them—not run from them. Give yourself permission for that departure and allow the challenges along the way to prepare you for your next flight. By doing this, you will develop strength. If you limit life's opportunities and take action only when you are assured success, you will be flying around the traffic pattern only on clear days for the rest of your life. The objective in this classroom called life is to learn and grow. Expose yourself to as many learning moments as possible in pursuit of your dreams.

*"The only real mistake is the one
from which we learn nothing."*
~Henry Ford

STEP BEYOND YOUR COMFORT ZONE

I WAS NEVER one to demand straight A's for my kids. Of course I wanted them to try and do the best they could. But when the *grade* becomes the focus verses the *education*, human nature is to take classes that are easier to maintain that grade. If you fear getting a low grade, there is one way to assure you don't—take easier classes. Easy is not the road to success.

This is the same with life. If you are afraid to take that promotion because you might fail, or are afraid to publish your book because you will be judged, you limit yourself.

If you don't push yourself, how will you get better, stronger, and faster? Is it possible to be the best you can be if you never make an error? Can you achieve success if you play it safe and never push your limits? Can you ever win if you don't get into the game?

> *"I have not failed.*
> *I've just found 10,000 ways that won't work."*
> ~Thomas A. Edison

MAKE FRIENDS WITH YOUR FAILURES—
THEY ARE YOUR BEST TEACHERS

FAILURE IS NOT an, *if*—it's a *when*. Since you will fail at something you might as well go for the gusto. The only way to succeed in life is if you are willing to fall on your face. Prepare yourself the best you can, and then go forth. Failing along the way is nothing more than paving your runway to success with lessons learned, and building unlimited resilience. In an attempt to make a super strong adhesive, Dr. Silver Spencer's failure ended up becoming Post-it Notes. Harland Sanders at the age of 60 had to close his restaurant. At 65, he decided to create a franchise, but was turned down 1,009 times before someone believed in his concept of what we know as KFC.

YOU CAN ONLY FAIL IF YOU GIVE UP

"Failed plans should not be interpreted as a failed vision. Visions don't change, they are only refined. Plans rarely stay the same, and are scrapped or adjusted as needed. Be stubborn about the vision, but flexible with your plan."
-John C. Maxwell

MY GOOD FRIEND Sonja was hired by an International Airline and scheduled to be trained in the last class prior to a merger. To her dismay, they cancelled that class. Sonja was on the street with many other pilots. Subsequently she was hired by another airline. During that time a blessing came to her life in the form of a beautiful son. Sonja eventually upgraded to captain, but the struggles were many while being a pilot mom. Her husband was a pilot too, and two pilot parents meant passing the baby off at the gate between flights. One day Sonja called dismayed with thoughts of giving up. The struggle of most working mothers is fear we aren't doing our best, while we are trying to do it all, and so perfectly too.

Perfection is an Illusion.

Doing your best is being your best, and sharing that with your children. You will be faced with family and work obligations on this journey—one of your greatest challenges. But that challenge should not be met with giving up on your life. Sonja was a few years away from a "flow-up" to a major airline. She was also ten years from the stage where her son would come home from school and she would ask, "How was your day?"

"Fine."

"What did you do today?"

"Nothing."

"What do you want for dinner?"

"I don't care."

His friends would be more important and he would eventually go off to college and form a life of his own. Her husband would be flying, and she would be sitting home alone wondering what happened to her life.

Our responsibilities as parents are to make sure our children are safe, loved, secure, and have all their needs met. There is power in children learning that Mom can go and will return. They grow up secure. Sonja did not have to give up her job. She learned to manage it. As difficult as the struggle was, she cut her schedule, and these two working parents are raising a wonderful young man while they both work challenging jobs.

Sonja flowed up to the legacy carrier and just finished her checkout on the A320. She is living the dream that so many pilots desire because she did not quit when times grew tough. When her son is off to college, Sonja and her husband will be able to bid the same plane and fly to exotic locations around the world—the sweet reward of success.

There are times you will do your best and life will not pan out, as you wanted it to. Not being accepted for a job or granted an interview, are good examples. But when your failure is placed in the hands of someone else, take a closer look at that failure and who really owns it. I was turned down for a position with United Airlines early in my career. I was devastated, humiliated and angry. All the emotions that went with not being good enough for them, and having my life's dreams shot down. *How could they not want me?* I did everything I could, and my 'everything' was not good enough. Strength means moving forward, knowing if you did your best, and did not quit, you did great! Today I am very thankful my career went a different path. United Airlines did me a huge favor. What you perceive as failure may actually turn into your greatest success.

On this journey you will come across people in positions of power making decisions over your life. There will be times you want to stand up and fight for what is right based on principle. This is where careful evaluation comes into play—you may be right, but at what expense? My rendition of the serenity prayer: Grant me the serenity to accept the things beyond my control; courage to change the things I can; and the wisdom to know when the time is right to take action.

Have a little faith along your journey
—that too takes strength.

TAKE ACTION NOW

- Write down anything you consider a failure in your life.
- Write down the lessons learned from those events. Sometimes it may be nothing more than to never do that again. Perhaps you learned to be more prepared next time. Perhaps you learned that while you thought that was what you wanted, the Universe knew better than you.
- Watch the movie *Coach Carter*. Sometimes you have to fight for what's right. Not taking the easy road builds strength and ultimate success.

Strength is the inner wisdom to
have faith on the darkest days,
knowing the sun will shine again.
To persevere during life's challenges.
It's belief that anything is possible,
and the ability to get up after every fall.
Strength is resilience,
and your birthright.

Taxiing down the tarmac, the jetliner abruptly stopped, and then returned to the gate. After an hour-long wait, it finally took off. A concerned passenger asked the flight attendant, "What was the problem?" "The pilot was bothered by a noise he heard in the engine," explained the Flight Attendant. "They took a long time to fix it," the passenger said. The flight attendant said, "Oh no, it just took us a while to find a new pilot."

CHAPTER 16

SUCCESS

WELCOME TO YOUR FINAL DESTINATION!

"Success comes from knowing that you did your best to become the best that you are capable of becoming."
~John Wooden

"LADIES AND GENTLEMEN, this is your captain speaking. We have begun our initial descent to an island called Success. Please remain seated with your seat belt fastened for the remainder of the flight. On behalf of the entire flight crew and myself, we hope that your *Flight to Success* was enjoyable, and that your continued journey will be equally so. For those of you who think you've reached your final destination, enjoy Success while you're here. There are many islands to visit, but an agent will be standing by to book your next destination. For those who landed at the wrong airport, please see the gate agent for connecting flights."

Success is the Journey

Every story of success in this book was not the end of the journey. The stories, adventures, and life challenges were just waypoints in the process called life—the journey. Love, loss, creation, and life continue to flow within each individual in this book, and will do so as long as they can breathe. The successes we shared were not the end, but the beginning. More books will be written, mountains climbed, airplanes built, love, loss, laughter and tears. The journey called life is not over until it's over.

Just because you reached your dream does not mean that was your final destination. Perhaps you got sidetracked and ended up someplace you thought you wanted to be, but now want off the island. When you give your all to a vision and get there, but it doesn't make you happy—you *can* leave. You *must* leave if you want to live a life of success. This is different from bailing out because life gets tough. This is about a change of heart. I am not professing to drop your accounting class because you don't like it. You need that course for a credit and there is a purpose for being there. I'm talking about picking a goal, getting there and saying, "Now what?" Then finding the courage to go for whatever it is you want, again. Find that courage. When you look forward to change, life becomes an adventure.

The truth is, when you reach your goal, you *will* want more because you have changed along the journey. We all do. And while change is one of the greatest and most exciting of all life events, it often receives the most resistance. When you are open to it, life unfolds in incredible ways. Allow those changes to take you to the next level.

THE SECRET OF SUCCESS

THE SECRET OF success is moving toward something and allowing the sky to open for you as you fly through it. The secret *within* success is enjoying each moment of your life. The secret *to* success is the journey. Build a life you love daily. The prize(s) will be there at the end of each day; have fun searching for them.

If you invest a fortune for school to become an attorney and later realize that the life of an attorney is not for you—get out. Don't stay because you are heavily invested in time and money. Use that education as a valued experience, then find your passion. Successful people don't bemoan the time and money they spent, they press on. The money is gone and time has been spent, but the experience is yours to keep and use for the next adventure.

It takes courage to move on after you've realized you landed at the wrong airport. Jennifer Lesher left a six-figure Microsoft job, at the age of 48, to pursue a dream of becoming an airplane mechanic. She doesn't even know if she will have a job after she finishes school. Fearless and powerful she presses forward to the unknown—the next dream. Marc Medley went from teacher to principal, creates music and hosts a live radio show, *The Reading Circle.*

Achieving your dreams will bring joy and satisfaction. But achievement is not the end of the flight. Embrace those feelings and dream again. When you reach your goal, there will be another destination. Life is about movement, creation, passion and joy. Life is a journey. Challenge, struggle, building strength, and conquering fear will open doors. Commitment and dedication with a strategy moves you forward. Learning from others and listening to the messages life is sending your way are tools to carry with you. Knowing yourself—who you are, what you want, and why you want it—will help to get you on a plane heading in the right direction. Be confident and ignite that passion so your dreams become a *must*. Manage your time wisely and everything you imagined can be yours.

YOU ARE THE HERO OF YOUR STORY!

WHEN I BEGAN writing novels, I had an epiphany about life. I realized we are all living a life parallel to a hero's journey in the stories we read. The hero in any novel is living an ordinary life until they are hit with an inciting incident—a call to adventure. When the hero accepts the calling, when you decide there is something you must accomplish in this life, the journey begins. In the first part of the story, a compelling reason will emerge, and the hero becomes committed. And so will you.

Once you make that commitment to push forward, exactly like the hero in any story, life will throw challenges your way. Do you quit or keep going? Stories are not written where the hero quits because life becomes too hard. The hero perseveres and becomes fully committed—there is nothing that will stop her. *What will stop you?*

At the end of the story, when the hero reaches her goal, she experiences a character arc—the hero changed along the way. She grew, and is now prepared for the next adventure in the series. You, too, will reach your goal as long as you do not quit. You will also change and become ready for the next adventure in your series called life.

That inciting incident in your life may be a voice, a thought, or an inspiration, something in your gut that says you belong someplace else. It might be a nine-year-old girl telling you that you cannot become a pilot because you're a girl, or dissatisfaction with the career you've chosen. Whatever it is, your journey has begun. You will face struggles along the way, and you will grow just like the hero in any story.

You joined me on this journey to success. But success as a destination is an illusion; so many think that when they get there they will be happy.

Happy is right here, right now, living the journey.

A multitude of people are searching for something they do not clearly understand. Hollywood is filled with rich people pumping drugs into their bodies and killing themselves. They have it all, but they are not happy. Senior captains complain about the job they once would have given anything to get. Plastic surgery is a billion dollar industry because wealthy people want to look better on the outside, because they don't feel good on the inside.

People reach their goals and are not happy because success is not what they imagined. What do you imagine success looks like? Is it a destination or a way to live right now?

How do you define success?

SUCCESS AND MONEY. I flew with a check airman who, adding to his already healthy paycheck, received an additional compensation for the students he flew with as an instructor pilot. He told me how he worked the system to fly and earn a pay-credit for an average of 130 hours per month. As if this wasn't enough, he tells his fellow crew members about his wealthy wife. But it gets better—he takes money from other pilots and flight attendants.

Crewmembers often dine together on layovers, each chipping in for their share of the bill. This captain purchases the most expensive meal, drinks the most expensive wine, suggests we all split the bill and never pays his share, or he removes the tip from the table. What makes him behave this way? His view of success is obviously wealth accumulation. He may have money, but I ask—at what cost? Spending so much time on the road away from his family—where is his joy? When will there ever be enough money? We all know the answer to that—there won't. History is filled with billionaires and corporate executives filling their pockets at the expense of others. Money is great, but how much is enough to make you happy if you sacrifice your life and values for it?

> *"Do what you love and the money will follow."*
> ~Marsha Sinetar

As a young child I had said, "I want to be rich *and* famous." Then I quickly added, "I really want to be famous, I don't care about the rich part." My values have changed. Now I could not care less about the famous part, either. I want experience and education and the ability to use that to help others. With that said, money would be fun, but the dollar has never been my driving force, just a result of hard work as I live my life with passion. It's okay to want money—the want is not a sin. The money is not a sin. The dollar may be a scorecard to validate the success of a business. However, money is not a valid scorecard for the quality of your life.

Dollars sitting in the bank might bring you security, but they won't make you happy. My 'wanting to be famous' days were an issue with identity and wanting acknowledgement of my existence. I felt unnoticed in my large family and the notoriety sounded great. My driving force changed when I understood myself and learned what was important.

Whatever drives you, use it to give you the momentum you need. But know who you are and why you want the goal. You will change as you grow; be open to that change. Change is a wonderful gift—make sure you open that package.

REACHING YOUR GOAL

REACHING YOUR GOAL often leaves a hole and an empty spot. After I accomplished something—attained the job I wanted, finished a degree, published a book, painted my house… that was all good and I felt proud, but the feelings of accomplishment were not lasting and I had always thought something was missing. I wanted more and could not feel sustained excitement for my accomplishments. In search of something, I was sure when I found it I would *be there*, and not want more.

Another life epiphany hit—success is not a destination, it's the journey, and I was never going to be a *there*. Success is having the guts to break through your fears, and make the impossible a reality. It means living your life to the fullest, despite others trying to make you a puppet. Success is not reaching a goal, but enjoying the journey on the way to your dreams. Goal attainment is a time to celebrate, to fill up your fuel tank, and move on to the next adventure. It is not the end of the journey but a step toward the next dream. Success is living a life filled with love, joy, passion, happiness, fulfillment and gratitude.

Success is the way you live—with passion and joy, while flying toward a goal. It is something you can taste, feel, and look forward to each day you open your eyes.

SUCCESS IS A CHOICE

SUCCESS IS WHEN you can look at each obstacle in your path as a learning opportunity. We don't always get what we want, but we always get what we need. Choose to believe you will reach your goal. You have the choice to change destinations if you find yourself at the wrong place. The choice to smile and embrace each day with whatever comes your way is within your power.

The Universe will throw obstacles in your path. It is up to *you* to decide if those challenges will destroy your life or make you stronger. Only you have the choice how events will impact you.

"Wow! I accomplished this. What's next?"

When you get to your destination, you can find another. Do not worry about the money and time spent, if you've enjoyed the journey and that journey brought you to this moment, you did great! You are living your life to the fullest.

Success is not a destination. Success is not something that you have to wait for in the future. Success is something you can have right at this moment. Success is about the journey—it's all about the flight.

FULFILLMENT LOVE INTEGRITY GRATITUDE HAPPINESS TRUST

FULFILLMENT

"I have wandered all my life, and I have also traveled; the difference between the two being this, that we wander for distraction, but we travel for fulfillment."
                                        ~Hilaire Belloc

A SUCCESSFUL JOURNEY is about contentment—finding joy wherever you are, and being present in the moment. Fulfillment comes from knowing that if you were to die tomorrow, you have lived *your* life and it was great. It means pursuing goals because you *want* to, not because you *need* to in order to fill a void or because someone thinks that you should accomplish more or something different than you are. For me, success means being happy to hang out with my husband and play scrabble, sitting on the floor with my grandkids, or making a really good landing.

LOVE

> *"Love is life. And if you miss love, you miss life."*
> ~Leo Buscaglia

LOVE IS NOT about what we get, but what we give. Love can bring the greatest joy, a thousand tears and the most painful heartaches. But love is so worth the pain and something you do not want to miss in your life. At the end of the day, with all the success in the world, if you don't have love, what do you have? If you haven't loved until it hurts, you have not lived.

One of the secrets of success is also learning how to love yourself, which in turn opens the door for others to love you, too. There is a reason we tell passengers to put on their oxygen masks first and then help others. Self-love is not feeding the ego. It's about knowing who you are, being comfortable with that person, and taking care of yourself because you are worth it. When you become secure with who you are, comfortable in your own skin, you will open the doors to love.

Love is about letting your guard down and not fearing being vulnerable. Open up and realize we all want the same thing—to be loved.

INTEGRITY

"The greatness of a man is not in how much wealth he acquires, but in his integrity and his ability to affect those around him positively."
~Bob Marley

WE HAVE ALL known or heard about someone who has achieved great success but lacked integrity. At what cost would you be willing to take from another to build your own fortune? At the end of the day would those actions make you proud? Could you feel success when you cheat the game of life for money?

My husband and I play scrabble and while we do, I'm often working on my computer between turns. One night I found a program that I could type in my letters and it would produce seven letter words. I thought it would be funny to do this and see when he noticed my increased performance. Despite doing it for a joke, after about three words I said, "Stop, I can't do this!" There was no fun playing a game that enables you to win without effort. Cheating does not give you the juice of reward that comes from succeeding at a goal.

Living a life with integrity, unwilling to push others under the bus no matter the cost, is more important to me than making a dollar at another's expense.

Live a life with integrity and live a life worth living.

GRATITUDE

"Gratitude is the healthiest of all human emotions.
The more you express gratitude for what you have,
the more likely you will have even more to express gratitude for."
                                                    -Zig Ziglar

SETTING UP YOUR day for success begins with being grateful for all you have in your life. One difference between those that achieve success and those that do not is their level of gratitude. People who are in the race to win the most toys can never be satisfied with what they have because they always want more. Living a life filled with a pursuit of goals only works if you're grateful for where you are today. If you miss the joy of your rewards along the way, you miss life.

You can be grateful where you are today. Think of three people who you feel gratitude that they are in your life. Smile. Feel the love and think about how great life is because they are there. Think about the meal you just ate. Was it a full sit down dinner or an apple while sitting under a tree?

Feeling gratitude slows you down so you can enjoy the moments of your life. In the process you become aware of how wonderful life is. Life *is* wonderful no matter your station or position. Everything we have was once a dream. If you don't have money for a huge meal, you can feel gratitude in that morsel of bread. When you appreciate what you have, more will come your way. We get what we focus on in life, and this includes gratitude. Be grateful for every breath you take, and the life you have been blessed to live.

HAPPINESS

> *"Happiness doesn't depend on any external*
> *conditions, it is governed by our mental attitude."*
>   ~Dale Carnegie

THERE IS A central theme in our journey to success—choice. Happiness is not exempt from that theme. Success in life is about attitude, and attitude is a choice. You can decide to be happy or unhappy. Happiness comes from within and is your birthright. You do not need external conditions or people to make you happy. Happiness is yours and you have control over it.

Since you have the choice, why wouldn't you choose to be happy?

Successful people are the heroes of their own stories; not the victims. They look at obstacles as challenges. They take responsibility for their actions and they laugh at their humanness. They make the choice to be happy. Besides, it is kind of fun smiling when the world is falling apart—makes people wonder what you are up to.

TRUST

> *"Trust yourself. Create the kind of self that you will be*
> *happy to live with all your life. Make the most of yourself*
> *by fanning the tiny, inner sparks of possibility into flames of*
> *achievement."*
>   ~Golda Meir

ON THE *Flight to Success* blog, I was asked what was the greatest challenge in my aviation career. I smiled. I might have said it was starting over so many times—I would have been wrong because that was fun. Perhaps it was navigating a flying career and motherhood at the same time, which would be true; but we all learned so much from the experience. What was my greatest challenge?

This question made me think of the *universal* challenge for all pilots, or for anyone who is chasing a dream—patience. Trusting and having patience, knowing that your dreams will become reality because you are doing what it takes to make them happen is essential. People with dreams want them to happen yesterday. Having patience is a virtue and one that will result in success.

You must believe—trust—that all will work out. Belief is a powerful equation in the success formula. Believe in yourself. Believe in your dreams. You must have faith that life will work out, as it should. As long as you are doing your part by participating, your time will come. Trust that you will get where you are going, and that arrival will propel you to the next destination. Have faith in the process of life. Enjoy today and be patient for tomorrow. Life will come, but success can be yours at this very moment.

Enjoy the Journey!

-XOX Karlene

Acknowledgment and References

Be Willing to Accept Help

ONE OF MY greatest challenges has been accepting help from others because I do not want to put anyone out. But when we don't allow others to help us, we are keeping them from sharing their gifts. I am learning to accept help when offered. Two angels, Jeffrey Roher and Carol Singleton stepped into my life and offered to edit this book, out of the graciousness of their hearts. I am ever grateful for their time, effort, and eye for perfection.

JEFFREY L. ROEHR was facing his own personal challenges, fighting major health issues, and yet he created time to read and provide valuable suggestions to *Flight to Success*. I am so grateful and appreciative for his help. As a million mile traveler, he also writes an aviation travel blog that is well-worth the read: https://paxview.wordpress.com Thank you JR for taking your time to read and edit, and the fun dialogue that followed.

CAROL SINGLETON picked up *Flight For Control* at the Western Washington Aviation Fair in 2012. In 2014, *Flight For Safety* had been rushed to market to make the same conference. Carol not only picked up her copy, but after the conference she spent her personal time and edited *Flight For Safety* and sent me the revision. When she said she wanted to help with the next book, too, I said, "You're hired!" Her reply was, *"I would love to proof your next book (and any others). You wouldn't need to pay me. I would enjoy supporting you on your mission. I'm not a trailblazer, but I have greatly enjoyed being behind those who are."* Thank you Carol for working this into your incredibly busy holiday, work schedule. There is never a good time, and you made it happen despite all obstacles, and I am every grateful.

LEARN TO ASK FOR HELP

DOING IT ALL does not have to mean doing it all by yourself. I had just arrived home from being out of town for five days, and prepared for a solid week of work. However, due to a family crisis, I ended up with a new quarter of graduate school beginning, editing and formatting this book, and babysitting three grandchildren during the same week. Priorities put family first. A similar time-crunch occurred when *Flight For Safety* was in the final stages and I had far too many balls in the air, but worked to do it all myself. Learning from the past has helped my future.

This time I not only realized that I did not have time to do it all, but I could ask for help. What a novel idea! I emailed my favorite publisher, Nathan Everett at elderroadbooks@outlook.com. He has a variety of services from editing, design and layout to full publishing. He had time available. If I could change anything in my life, it would have been getting domestic help while the children were young, instead of trying to be superwoman. Life is about learning and growing. It only took me 52 years to take action on this lesson. Thank you Nathan for being there in my time of need.

LAUGHTER IS THE BEST MEDICINE

MARC EPNER has a heart of gold and soars with the eagles
when he's not cracking the world up with his humor. I met him
at Aviation Universe in Chicago during a radio event, as he is a
co-host of simple flight radio: http://www.simpleflight.net/radio.
html Marc shared a joke with us that his mother had sent him (I
know where he get's his humor) and realized I needed laughter in
Flight to Success. We plotted for many months and shared jokes
via email. While the jokes in this book have been modified many
times, I have no idea who the original authors are. However, I
would like to give credit to Marc for bringing laughter to our life.

MEET THE HEROES OF THIS STORY

ANDREW HARTLEY is a certificated flight instructor and commercial pilot in Columbus, Ohio. While he lost his medical, he *will
be* medically certified again. "Whatever it takes." You can reach
Andrew at http://smartflighttraining.com

BO CORBY is a retired airline captain who continues to pursue
flying opportunities and maintains currency in the King Air and
Pilatus PC-12. Air Mentor, his flight school at Boeing Field continues to seek out hopefuls who have a passion for aviation and want
to bypass all the mistakes he made as a young and fearless (but very
lucky) young pilot. Bo may be contacted at borhino@aol.com or
206 769-3398. *"Only those with a burning fire to stay alive and be
the best there is need apply."*

HEATHER MCCORKLE, Author of fantasy & historical fiction, is
a graphic designer who will help bring your book to life, and an
ISF (Ian Somerhalder Foundation) volunteer. She can be reached
at http://heathermccorkle.wix.com/heathermccorkle

JANINE SHEPHERD is the best selling author of *Never Tell Me Never, The Gift Of Acceptance, On My Own Two Feet, Dare to Fly,* and *Reaching For Stars.* She is an international speaker, change expert, and aerobatics pilot. She can be reached at http://www.janineshepherd.com

JEAN DENIS MARCELLIN, the Author of *The Pilot Factor,* is a captain for a major Canadian charter company and aircraft management business. His passion for Crew Resource Management and life experience flows into his company, Plane&Simple Solutions, where he teaches effective leadership and communication skills to the student pilot and airline professional. He can be located at http://www.planesimplesolutions.com and jd.marcellin@planesimplesolutions.com

JENNIFER LESHER is a novelist, blogger, mountain biker, travel junkie, and armchair philosopher. She recently left her job in the software industry to pursue certification as an airplane mechanic, which she will receive in April 2015. To read her blog, learn more about her novel, *Raising John* and the upcoming sequel, visit her website: http://jenniferlesherauthor.com

JESSICA COX is a motivational speaker and disability activist. She is the star and producer of the documentary, *Right Footed,* about her life and challenges. To check out the inspiring film and to contact Jessica to book a speaking engagement, you can contact her at http://jessicacox.com

KALIMAR AVILA-PETITT (eldest daughter) has been international Executive IT Recruiter for the last 10 years and presently works with CyberCoders. She is the mother of three, and actively involved in her community; she is currently the President of the local PTA and manages additional leadership roles. She can be contacted at: Kalimar@cybercoders.com

KAYLA, DR. WOSPSCHALL (middle daughter) is the mother of two, an Archaeologist, Science Educator and Artist. She can be contacted at Kwopschall@gmail.com

KRYSTA WOGEN, (youngest daughter) is a mother of two, teacher and a nutrition/fitness coach. If you have health, diet, or weight challenges, she can be reached at KrystaWogen@gmail.com

LELAND SHANLE (CHIP) is the owner of Broken Wings Productions. He is also a pilot and the award winning author of *Project Seven Alpha*, *Vengeance at* Midway and Guadalcanal, *ENDGAME in the Pacific* and *Code Name INFAMY*. You can contact him at http://lelandshanle.com

MARC MEDLEY is a principal responsible for more than 500 students in a K-8 elementary school in the school district of Paterson, New Jersey. He is the host of *The Reading Circle* book talk radio program, heard live on Saturday mornings from 6:00 a.m.–7:00 a.m. Eastern Time on WP88.7 FM and at Gobrave.org. Marc can be contacted at http://www.thereadingcircle01.com

MARK L. BERRY is an airline pilot, creative writer, lyricist, contributing editor for *Airways* magazine, and the author of a memoir *13760 Feet—My Personal Hole in the Sky*. His memoir, song collaborations, and more can be found at http://marklberry.com

ROB AKERS is an honored military representative, airline pilot, husband, father and author of the *Solider Of God The Book of Lot*. He can be reached at http://robakers.wordpress.com

ROBERT DUGONI is a writer turned lawyer turned writer. He is an Amazon #1 and *New York Times* bestselling author, husband, father, dog lover and dreamer. His many novels include crime thrillers, mystery, and police procedural. He can be reached at http://robertdugoni.com

SONJA LOCKE is currently flying an A320 for an international airline. If you are facing the challenges of managing motherhood with an aviation career, please email her at mekcol@gmail.com

SYD BLUE is the owner and operator of an aviation business specializing in aerial surveillance. In addition to living a life in the skies, she has written *FlyGirl* and *Circle* to inspire young adults toward a passion for aviation. Syd can be reached at https://sydblue.com.

VICTOR WAGONER is a captain for international airline on the Airbus A330. Loving life, and happy to be flying. If you have a similar challenge and are looking for guidance, you can email Victor at VeWag2@gmail.com

WILLIAM BERNHARDT is a bestselling author, who leads a weekend writing workshop and teaches five-day writing seminars and master classes in various cities across the country. He is also available for public speaking. He can be contacted at: http://williambernhardt.com

BOOK REFERENCES:

DUHIGG, C. (2012). *The Power of Habit.* New York, N.Y., Random House Trade Paperbacks.

GONZALES, L. (2003) *Deep Survival: Who Lives, Who Dies, and Why.* New York, N.Y., Norton & Company.

MARCELLIN, J. D. (2014). *The Pilot Factor.* Canada.

PETITT, K. (2012) *Flight For Control,* SeaTac Washington, Jet Star Publishing.

PETITT, K. (2014) *Flight For Safety,* SeaTac Washington, Jet Star Publishing.

ROBBINS, A. (1991). *Awaken The Giant Within: How to take immediate control of your mental, physical and emotional self.* New York, N.Y., Simon & Shuster.

SINGER, M. A. (2007). *The untethered soul, the journey beyond yourself.* Oakland CA., New Harbinger.

AVIATION THRILLERS BY KARLENE PETITT.

FLIGHT SERIES—

Flight For Control
Flight For Safety
Flight For Survival (Fall 2016)

CHILDREN'S BOOKS BY KARLENE PETITT

I Am Awesome (Spring 2015)
Grandma's Plane (Fall 2015)
Pigs Can Fly! (Fall 2015)

KARLENE IS AVAILABLE to host aviation discussion groups, join book clubs, or speak at your meetings.

Please email her at Karlene.Petitt@gmail.com to schedule your next event. And check out her blog at http://KarlenePetitt.com

ABOUT THE AUTHOR:

KARLENE PETITT IS currently an A330 International Airline pilot living in Seattle. She is type-rated on the B747-400, B747-200, B767, B757, B737, B727 and A330 aircraft. She holds MBA and MHS degrees, and is currently working on her PhD at Embry-Riddle Aeronautical University in Aviation, with a focus on safety. She has flown for Coastal Airways, Evergreen, Braniff, Guyana and Tower Air. She has instructed at America West Airlines, Premair, Guyana, and has also flown and instructed for an International Airline on the 747-400 and 747-200. She has spent 21 years training pilots, and has been instrumental in training program development at multiple airlines. She is a mother of three grown daughters and grandmother of seven.

CPSIA information can be obtained
at www.ICGtesting.com
Printed in the USA
FSOW01n1841260116
16120FS